SMART LEADERSHIP
Lessons *for* Leaders

Prof. M. S. Rao

STERLING PAPERBACKS
An imprint of
Sterling Publishers (P) Ltd.
A-59, Okhla Industrial Area, Phase-II, New Delhi-110020.
Tel: 26387070, 26386209; Fax: 91-11-26383788
E-mail: mail@sterlingpublishers.com
www.sterlingpublishers.com

Smart Leadership: Lessons for Leaders
© 2012, Prof. M. S. Rao
ISBN 978 81 207 7415 5

All rights are reserved.
No part of this publication may be reproduced, stored in a retrieval system or transmitted, in any form or by any means, mechanical, photocopying, recording or otherwise, without prior written permission of the author.

Printed in India
Printed and Published by Sterling Publishers Pvt. Ltd.,
New Delhi-110 020.

International Acclaim/Endorsements

"The international leadership guru, Professor M.S.Rao outlines essences of leadership lessons that help you become a smart leader. I strongly recommend this book."

Vijay Govindarajan
Among World's Top 3 Management Gurus

"In his book, **Smart Leadership – Lessons for Leaders**, international leadership guru, Professor M.S.Rao, gives us a curriculum for becoming 'smart leaders' – several lessons for achieving such status and excelling in this new role. Without having to enroll at your local university or college, you'll be treated to a brilliant 'guest lecture' in each chapter by some of the world's smartest leaders – Steve Jobs, Martin Luther King, Jr. and Peter Drucker just to name a few. In his 'six steps for success' within the book, Professor Rao gives us the key to enter the elite world of 'smart leaders.' He teaches us to have 'clarity of purpose first,' then to tackle his six steps, and ultimately, to unlock our secret potential."

Marshall Goldsmith
Author of The New York Times bestsellers,
MOJO and What Got You Here Won't Get You There

"*Smart Leadership* brings essential leadership lessons, not for the leaders of the past, but for the leaders of the future. Professor M.S. Rao's book will inspire, engage and move us to share its messages widely. Moreover, it's fun to read, to contemplate, and make it our own."

Frances Hesselbein
President & CEO, The Leader to Leader Institute
(Formerly The Peter F. Drucker Foundation for Nonprofit Management)
Former CEO, The Girl Scouts of the USA

"Professor M.S. Rao has compiled a thought-provoking treasury of leadership wisdom in this slim book, going to the heart of principles that support enlightened management practice. Of special value is his focus on cultivating skills that produce both success and broader significance. These are ideas that can create a better world."

Dipak C. Jain
Dean, INSEAD

"Professor M.S. Rao gives us the essential life principle to lead, live and achieve on a new level! Use the profound and practical tools in *Smart Leadership* to become a leader for life."

Kevin Cashman
Senior Partner, Korn/Ferry,
Author of the bestseller, Leadership from the Inside Out

"Professor M. S. Rao has again provided us with invaluable insight into the mysteries and complexities of leadership: *Smart Leadership – Lessons for Leaders* provides vital leadership intelligence for these very difficult and puzzling times."

Emmett C. Murphy
Author of The New York Times bestseller, Leadership IQ

"*Smart Leadership - Lessons for Leaders* is an invaluable resource for all leaders seeking personal and professional growth. Professor M. S. Rao's practical insights will help you reexamine the assumptions by which you lead and enhance your personal leadership brand."

Richard Chang
CEO, Richard Chang Associates, Inc.,
Author of The Passion Plan and The Passion Plan at Work

"Professor M. S. Rao's book *Smart Leadership – Lessons for Leaders* addresses one of the biggest crises of our time – the failure of more people to take responsibility for being a positive influence in this world. We need more people to step up and lead when they see a need, not wait for those in authority to do something. This book isn't just for designated leaders; it is for everybody!"

John Renesch
Author of The Great Growing Up: Being Responsible for Humanity's Future

"*Smart Leadership – Lessons for Leaders* is a unique and must have book for the developing leader, Professor M. S. Rao's distinctive perceptions provide details to make excelling as a smart leader, easy and effortless."

Arthur F. Carmazzi
Among world's Top Ten Leadership Guru and Founder of Directive Communication Psychology
Author of Lessons from the Monkey King – Leading Change to Create Gorilla Sized Results

"The international leadership guru, Professor M.S. Rao has come out with another leadership book *Smart Leadership – Lessons for Leaders*. This book is an endeavor to equip you with lessons that help you minimize your mistakes and enhance your leadership effectiveness. I strongly recommend this book."

Terri Levine
World's Top Ten Coaches and Author of Stop Managing Start Coaching and Sell Without Selling: Lessons from the Jungle for Sales Success.

"It is often said we learn from our mistakes and the mistakes of others and each of us are products of our past. This is true and it is up to each of us to not let our mistakes hold us back. We can learn from the others in order that we do not make the same mistakes. Before we can move forward we must be willing to let go of past mistakes. Everyone who reads this book needs to embrace the insights and advice in the wonderful book."

Lenny Laskowski
Author of the bestseller 10 Days to More Confident Public Speaking

Dedicated to
my friend
Sadhanala Surya Kumar
A good friend is a gift from God

Acknowledgments

A book is never the work of the author alone. Several quotes, examples and anecdotes in this book are the result of a collection from different sources. It is practically impossible to acknowledge each one of them separately. While I have tried to give credit wherever it is due, in case I have missed anything, I will give due credit in future editions if it is brought to my notice.

I thank the team of Sterling Publishers Pvt. Ltd., for publication of this book.

I express special thanks to all the readers who graciously took time off from their busy schedules to write to me, share their views, and offer feedback on my books *Soft Leadership: Make Others Feel More Important; Spirit of Indian Youth: Soft Skills for Young Managers; Stand Out! Build a Successful Career and Become a Global Leader; Smartness Guide: Success Tools for Students; Spot Your Leadership Style: Build Your Leadership Brand; Soft Skills: Enhancing Employability; Soft Skills for Students: Classroom to Corporate;* and *Secrets for Success: Failure is Only a Comma not a Full Stop.* I wholeheartedly thank you for your endless support and love.

Foreword

*Introduction to Smart Leaders:
A New Unified Model Of Leadership*
Fons Trompenaars[*]

This enlightening book reveals that one of the essential distinguishing characteristic of leaders in a turbulent environment is their propensity to reconcile seemingly opposing values. In contrast, managers (rather than leaders) seem to have solvable problems — "Next problem please".

Leaders are frequently suffering from insomnia because they were not able to resolve a dilemma they faced. It is difficult "not to have made it", but even more difficult not knowing "what to make". Then, even worse, the successful integration of conflicting values frequently leads to the creation of one or more new dilemmas. It is a continuous process.

What are these dilemmas that smart leaders face? Of course you have to inspire as a leader and you have also to listen. You need to follow the orders of HQ to fulfil the global strategy and you have to have local success by adapting to regional circumstances. You have to decide when to act yourself and also when and where to delegate.

---

[*] Founder, Trompenaars Hampden-Turner Intercultural Management Consulting

As a professional you need to input your own day-to-day contribution and at the same time to be passionate about the mission of the whole. And you need to simultaneously use your brilliant analytical power while enabling the contribution of others. You need to develop an excellent strategy while simultaneously having answers to when this strategy misses its goal.

The view of leadership taken here is that leaders find themselves *between* conflicting demands and are subject to an endless series of paradoxes and dilemmas. There are non-stop culture clashes and by culture we mean not simply the cultures of different nations, but those of different disciplines, functions, genders, classes, and so on. Professor M. S. Rao illustrates some well-known leadership dilemmas in this book, but their exact descriptions are less important than the capacity for paradoxical problem solving which underlies them all. These include the following examples:

- Blend both Hard and Soft Skills
- A Good Leader is a Great Servant
- Empower People Delegate Effectively
- Be a Transformational Leader
- Stay Calm in the Eye of the Storm vs Manage Uncertainty
- Articulate Your Vision Effectively vs. Emphasize on "Means", not "Ends"
- Learn and Grow Continuously vs. Use Your Time Effectively

The above are an army of current challenges. Are leaders the "authors" of strategy and policy or do they orchestrate the necessary participation? Do leaders deal in high-level abstractions or in concrete details? Can a leader be a servant also? Such questions culminate in what is, perhaps, the biggest crisis of the day. Are leaders people hired by shareholders to channel the lion's share of profits in their direction, or do they lead a learning, developing community?

We thus begin to understand why there are numerous definitions of good leadership. You read Warren Bennis and you find it is all about vision, mission and transparency. You go to the French literature and read how great leaders are functions of their educational background. Compare this with other regional literature that suggest you should be male, senior and from a particular college.

With the internationalization of organizations, we find that leaders have to face multi-cultural teams. What style of leadership is effective in those diverse circumstances? We submit that it requires a set of value-free competencies that we identify as trans-cultural competence.

Professor M. S. Rao identified that the significant and common factor amongst successful leaders today is their competence to reconcile seemingly opposing demands on a continuing basis. So what are these dilemmas that smart leaders face?

- Blend both Hard and Soft Skills

The neuro-linguistic anthropologist, Deborah Tannen, has described this as a clash between *Report* and *Rapport*. You can only *report* criticism to a subordinate if you have sufficient initial *rapport* with her. Tannen believes that women are more rapport oriented, while men are more report oriented. If she is right, then male supervisors may be delivering negative verdicts to female subordinates who are not yet prepared to trust them, because they feel that their rapport with this man is too weak. The situation can be charted as follows.

At bottom right we have the pseudo-gallantry with which male supervisors may reassure female supervisees falsely. At top left the criticism is too hard to take because the mutual respect and rapport is lacking. Only at top right is the female subordinate getting feedback that helps her to improve continuously and win deserved promotion.

Dilemma 1   Rapport — Report

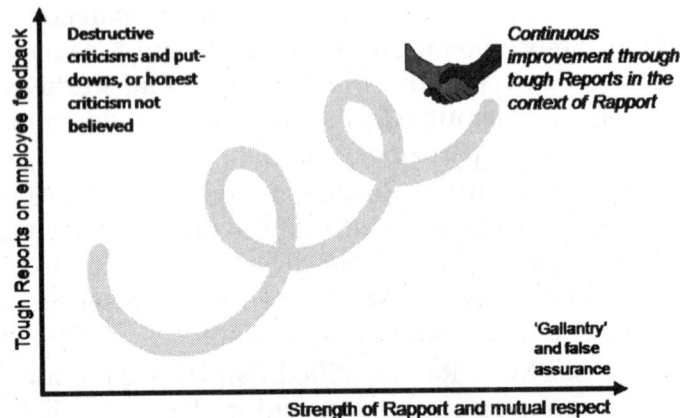

We see that if we achieve the 10/10 position in the top right hand corner we have created a relational context through soft skills within which we will give hard feedback through hard skills.

- A Good Leader is a Great Servant

In business, the concept of the "servant leader"[1] is appropriate wherever it is an inherent mission of the company to be innovative for customers. When any leader serves his or her subordinates, they are modelling how they should do likewise for customers. If the leader is not too proud or too high to serve others, why shouldn't employees imitate this by mirroring the behaviour? Servant leaders are forever trying to give away their status, only to get it back again through gratitude and admiration. The more you serve, the more you lead fellow servers.

Servant leadership is a powerful vehicle for the transition from the Family to Guided Missile culture. The leader "gives" followers more than they could conceivably repay; thus they become obligated and even more compliant to the

---

[1] Greenleaf, R.K. 1977/2002. The Power of Servant Leadership. Berrett-Koehler Publishers, Inc, San Francisco

leader's wishes. Is the servant leader at the bottom of a deep shaft, or at the apex of a truncated pyramid? The answer is "both". The leader has reversed the organizational hierarchy and is serving subordinates as if they were superiors. Our recent research reveals that the essential distinguishing characteristic of leaders in a multi-cultural environment is their propensity to reconcile seemingly opposing values. In contrast, managers (rather than leaders) seem to have solvable problems—"Next problem please".

Getting things done is important for a manager's performance. But doesn't the doing of vulgar and mundane things need to be in balance with our private life? As a leader you need also to be able to be yourself. However, from our research findings we conclude that our leaders are not different from what they do. They seem to be one with what they do. One of the most important sources of stress is when being and doing are not integrated. An overdeveloped achievement orientation that doesn't harmonize with what suits the persons in their lifestyle and themselves leads to ineffective behaviours.

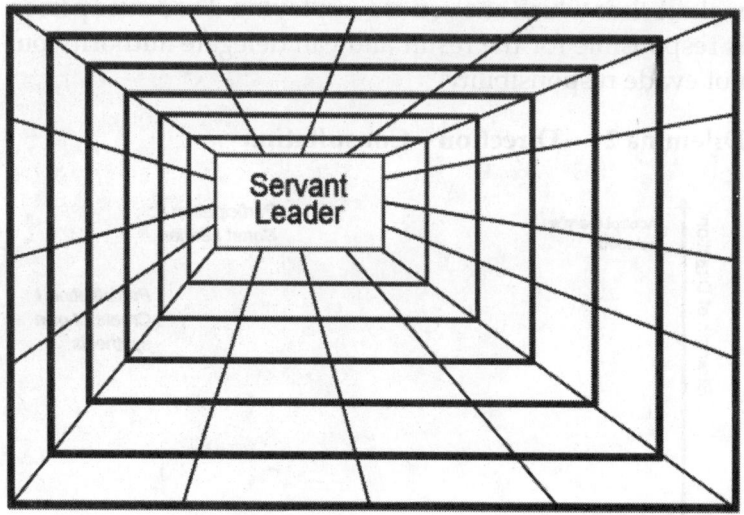

- Empower People, Delegate Effectively

In smart leadership we find the need for combining two styles of "participative leadership", that is, ways of combining top-down leadership influence with bottom-up group and team initiatives. In both cases leadership is legitimized by operating at a higher level of abstraction.

In participation I, subordinates contribute a large variety of inputs and the leader listens to all ideas and combines as many of these as possible in a higher level synthesis. Ideally subordinates see themselves and the reflection of their inputs in the leader's solution which encompasses multiple points of view.

In participation II, the leader outlines the challenge, describes the problem to be solved, and states what standards a solution must accomplish and what goals a solution must serve. He or she makes sure that team members have among them the necessary resources, informational and physical, and then leaves them to come up with solutions. The leader then endorses the best of these.

It is best *not* to muddle up these two approaches and to make it clear which one you are employing. The senior person is responsible for the result and can delegate authority but not evade responsibility.

Dilemma 2   Direction — Consultation

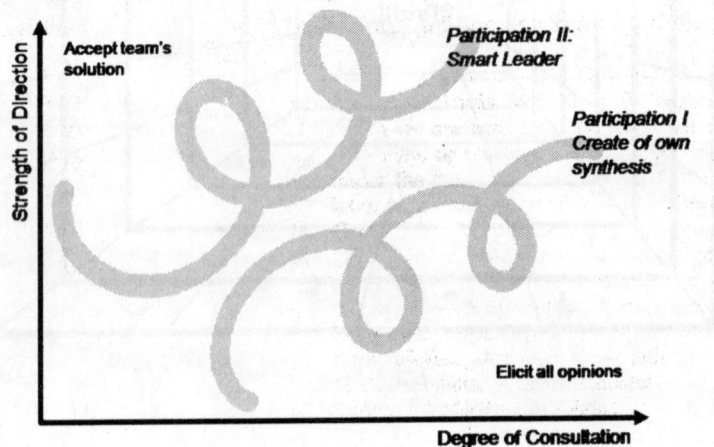

It is possible to train for both types of leadership. We have exercises in which many disparate ideas are thrown at would-be leaders and they can create their own syntheses and we have training in how to sponsor teams. How to issue a challenge? How to describe the team remit? How to give them enough but not too much autonomy?

- Be a Transformational Leader

James McGregor Burns differentiated transactional leadership from transformational leadership. In the transactional style, there is a simple exchange of work for money, or votes for representation. Nothing new is created, and each party serves only self-interest.

In the transformational style, the leader transforms the consciousness of those led, and by their response, those led transform the consciousness of the leader. Each elicits a potential latent in others and brings to fruition a yearning or aspiration of which they were not previously aware.

On one horn of the dilemma is the authority of the leader, which becomes corrupted by the unilateral exercise of power from which the populace shrinks. On the other horn is the degree of participation, which can lead to lost or abdicated leaders, whose authority is taken over by those who are supposed to lead. Between this arbitrary and failed leadership lies the transactional leader, as a kind of compromise, tolerated because they provide the necessities of life: routine work for routine pay. The reconciliation is the transformational leader, whose followers "stand on the shoulders of giants" and are elevated through having experienced them. In this last case we see that the individual reward of learning is offered to the larger team by its leaders. It is a very subtle reward structure which includes the learning of the individual through the group rather than at the cost of the group.

The following graph shows this clearly.

Transformational Leadership

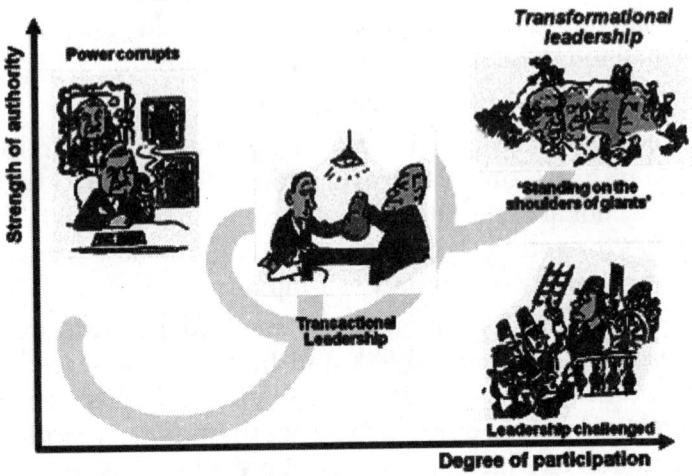

- Stay Calm in the Eye of the Storm vs Manage Uncertainty

Is a good leader a passionate person or rather a person who controls his or her display of emotions? We recognize two extreme types. Passionate leaders without reason are known as neurotics. Overly controlling leaders without emotions are known as robots or control freaks. Both types are unsuccessful in a multi-cultural environment. The success Richard Branson derives are because he continuously checks his passion with reason. If we consider the less emotive Jack Welsh, we observe a leader that gives meaning to his control by showing his passion at specific well-chosen moments.

Club Med's prodigious growth had overstrained its traditional management structure. It had become intoxicated by its self-celebrations, week after week, and was not keeping track of costs or logistics. The company's downward spiral had begun and now chronic under- investment made it worse. The company was not competent in the more neutral hard side of the business (travel, finance, logistics etc.) Resorts were not profit centers, and several had lost money without anyone realizing it. Many opened too early in the season or not early enough. Moreover, hospitality had simply been increased with no awareness of diminishing returns. The food and wine expenditure had escalated.

- Articulate Your Vision Effectively vs Emphasize on 'Means', not 'Ends'

A smart leader contrasts two sources of experienced control: that from inside us, inner-directed, visionary and that from outside us, outer- and means-directed. Strategy, for example, could be designed from within top management, or it could emerge from the company's interface with customers, outside top management. We argue that these processes are integratable. Top management could use its inner resources to design and reshape the strategies emerging outside, which had already pleased customers. We called this *crafted strategy*, in honour of Henry Mintzberg, as when the clay rises spontaneously from the rotating potter's wheel.

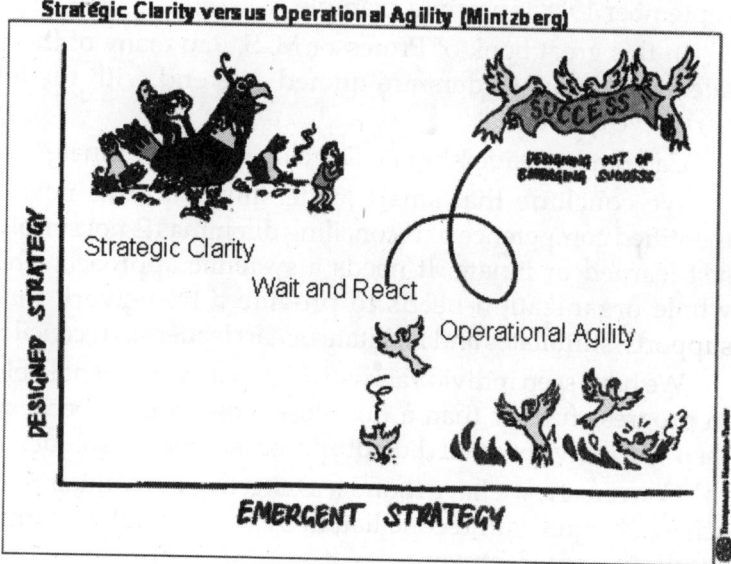

- Learn and Grow Continuously vs Use Your Time Effectively

The zero mistake ideal for using your time more effectively has been abandoned. In the car industry the only way to maintain your relationship with the client is to give good service after the malfunctioning of your car. With smart leadership serial failure is the path to ultimate success. You learn by successive approximation to what you have idealized. In many cases, learning by error or failure may be the only way to continuously improve. After all, the very words for failure and success are relative. If you aim very high or innovate boldly you are bound to fail more often, so that "failure" may be the consequence of high aspiration while success may be the consequence of low aspiration. Moreover it is often quicker to learn by mistakes and correct these than to calculate at length and get it right first time. It is certainly more dramatic, more memorable and more vivid to endure failure as a prelude to success. It has been truly said that we learn most from negative feedback, from what we did not expect. Fleming's discovery and isolation of penicillin in September 1928 is a prime example.

In this great book of Professor M. S. Rao many of these talents of smart leaders are quoted. We end with the all pervasive question

Can Smart Leadership Be Developed Or Is It Innate?

We conclude that smart leadership with this newly identified competence of reconciling dilemmas is not simply just learned or innate. It needs a systemic approach. The whole organization needs to provide a framework that supports, stimulates and facilitates smart leaders to reconcile.

We have seen individuals with high potential, yet not able to progress further than a (lose-lose) compromise because their work environment did not appreciate creative solutions.

Conversely, we have found less effective individuals that achieved significant reconciliation by their stimulating and supportive environment.

How to create such an environment? It begins with smart leaders who practice what they preach. And it is of utmost importance that rewards are created that motivate individuals and teams to do so.

Our message is to link smart leadership to business issues and business results and make it into a continuous process so that it becomes a way of living rather than a conceptual exercise.

I wish you lots of reading fun.

2 January, 2012

Preface

"Experience is a hard teacher because she gives the test first, the lesson afterwards"

Vernon Sanders Law

Welcome to *Smart Leadership – Lessons for Leaders*! You may be wondering why I am publishing another book on leadership. Leadership is my passion and I enjoy teaching, training, and writing books on leadership to help build more leaders who make a difference to this world.

In one of my previous books on leadership, I had highlighted the different leadership styles for the reader to select from and follow. In another book, I had emphasized the need for Soft Leadership to manage the complexities in the corporate world. In this book I have outlined several rules to excel as a smart leader.

The book starts with Martin Luther King Jr, who achieved what was considered impossible in those times. It explains Operation Geronimo and outlines the leadership lessons we can learn from Barack Obama. The book pays a tribute to the legendary Steve Jobs for following the road less travelled. It describes the servant leader Florence Nightingale. It presents Ram Charan's *Leaders at all Levels,* Jim Collins' *Level 5 Leadership* and John Maxwell's *Leadership Ladder of 5 levels of leadership*. It outlines leadership lessons from Peter Drucker, the father of modern management. It concludes with Marshall Goldsmith's message from *What Got You Here Won't Get You There*.

This book will serve as an inspiration to enhance your leadership effectiveness and help you to achieve success. I have learnt some of these lessons from the books I read and some during my 30 years of diverse experience in defense, teaching, training, research, and consultancy.

I am confident that you will enjoy reading these success stories and case studies, learn the lessons, and excel as a smart leader.

Professor M. S. Rao

Contents

Acknowledgments vi
Foreword vii
Preface xix

1. Introduction — 1
2. You Are the Leader! — 8
3. Leadership Lessons from Barack Obama — 15
4. Leadership is not a Popularity Contest — 21
5. Be a Leader, Not a Boss — 24
6. Articulate Your Vision Effectively — 28
7. Follow the Road Less Travelled — 35
8. Emphasize "Means", not "Ends" — 43
9. Manage Uncertainty — 49
10. Stay Calm in the Eye of the Storm — 53
11. Use Your Time Effectively — 59
12. Delegate Effectively — 66
13. Empower People — 74
14. Be Open to Feedback — 78
15. Blend both Hard and Soft Skills — 84
16. Humility Goes Before Honour — 88
17. A Good Leader is a Great Servant — 92
18. Learn and Grow Continuously — 97
19. Be a Transformational Leader — 100

20	Build Leaders around You	108
21	Live Your Life Completely	115
22	Make a Difference to the Lives of Others	120
23	Soar like an Eagle	125
	Bibliography	129
	Glossary	131
	Index	135

1

Introduction

"If any of you are around when I have to meet my day, I don't want a long funeral. And if you get somebody to deliver the eulogy, tell them not to talk too long. . . . Tell them not to mention that I have a Nobel Peace Prize, that isn't important. Tell them not to mention that I have three or four hundred other awards, that's not important. . . . I'd like somebody to mention that day, that Martin Luther King Jr tried to give his life serving others. I'd like for somebody to say that day, that Martin Luther King Jr tried to love somebody. . . . I want you to say that I tried to love and serve humanity."

Dr Martin Luther King

The Man Who Moved the Mighty

Dr Martin Luther King Jr was one of the most inspiring leaders, who touched the world through his courage and convictions. He was a symbol of right as against might and proved to the world that it is the right that wins at the end of the day rather than the might.

It was very difficult to lead a Civil Rights movement in America in those days, when whites dominated and

Dr Martin Luther King Jr

discriminated against blacks. He was courageous enough to take on the mighty through the right means and methods. Although there have been a number of courageous leaders in the past, Dr King is still remembered for his amazing and exemplary leadership.

Dr King was one of the youngest leaders to achieve fame and success. At 33 he led the Civil Rights movement in America. At 34 he delivered the famous speech *I have a Dream*. At 35 he won the Nobel Peace Prize. At 39 he was assassinated. He achieved such a lot by the young age of 39, brought revolutionary changes within the American society and made a great impact globally with his principles of peace and non-violence by following the footsteps of Mahatma Gandhi.

Dr King was a visionary who led from the front and used words skilfully to connect with his people. He was a transformational leader who changed the American society by bringing an end to racial segregation and discrimination. He was named the Man of the Year by Time magazine in 1963 and became not only the symbolic leader of American blacks, but also a global leader. He is truly a legend who showed exemplary and amazing leadership when odds were stacked against him and, that too, through non-violent and peaceful means. Here are the lessons we can learn from his leadership:

Leadership Lessons from Dr King

"If a man is called to be a street sweeper, he should sweep streets even as Michelangelo painted, or Beethoven composed music, or Shakespeare wrote poetry. He should sweep streets so well that all the host of heaven and earth will pause to say, 'Here lived a great street sweeper who did his job well.'"

- He believed in his values and principles. Despite facing innumerable threats to his life and being subjected to several abuses, he did not give up his Civil Rights movement. He remarked, "I believe that unarmed truth and unconditional love will have the final word in reality. This is why right, temporarily defeated, is stronger than evil triumphant."
- He had excellent communication skills. He knew how to mould and articulate his vision effectively. His speech *I have a Dream* is one of the finest motivational speeches in the world and raises the key issues regarding equality of blacks with whites.
- He was highly committed and dedicated to his cause. He travelled far and wide and delivered speeches on his firm commitment to the cause of the rights of the blacks.
- He shared whatever he had. He shared the prize money from the Nobel Prize with others for furtherance of the Civil Rights movement.
- He said, "I have a dream that my four little children will one day live in a nation where they will not be

judged by the colour of their skin, but by the content of their character." His dream was fulfilled and this made a huge difference to the lives of the blacks and the oppressed.

Learning Lessons

"Whenever you make a mistake or get knocked down by life, don't look back at it too long. Mistakes are life's way of teaching you. Your capacity for occasional blunders is inseparable from your capacity to reach your goals. No one wins them all, and your failures, when they happen, are just part of your growth. Shake off your blunders. How will you know your limits without an occasional failure? Never quit. Your turn will come."—Og Mandino

It is a fact that life is a series of lessons which have great value, provided we learn from them. Do not panic during the difficult times in your life. These situations make you tough and should draw the best out of you. Do not get dejected. Observe and analyse closely what went wrong, learn from it, and move on.

Leaders learn from multiple sources such as from observation, teaching, training, experience, interaction, evaluation, and feedback. They also learn by studying other successful leaders. Though leadership is not something that can be learned by reading books alone, reading books will help to minimize mistakes and maximize outcomes. Smart leaders learn the techniques of leadership quickly and acquire the tools and skills to lead others effectively.

What is Smart Leadership?

Leaders like Jeff Immelt of General Electric, Michael Dell of Dell Computers, and Steve Jobs of Apple Computers have one thing in common, that is, they are all smart leaders. For Jeff Immelt, taking over as CEO of General Electric was really a challenging task because people had huge expectations after Jack Welch had led the company successfully for many years. Jeff managed to establish his credentials through smart leadership. Both Michael Dell and Steve Jobs faced tough competition and managed their companies successfully through smart, innovative strategies during the recession.

Smart leadership is a blend of both soft and hard skills, and soft and hard power. It effectively links both hard and smart work. Smart leadership can be defined as the process of setting goals, influencing people, building effective teams, motivating people, and, finally, aligning their energies and efforts towards organizational goals and objectives both through soft and hard skills as well as soft and hard power.

Smart leaders possess presence of mind and are tactful in dealing with people. They have the art of leading and managing the emotions and egos of their people. They are ready to perform the role of a manager or a leader, as the situation demands. They are smart in learning lessons quickly from the mistakes of others and leveraging on the experience of others. They believe in quality performance and results. They display entrepreneurial skills, believe in innovation and creativity, possess flexibility and adaptability, and possess many skills like communication skills, team building skills, cross cultural skills, presentation skills, empathy, and humility, to name a few. In brief, they are smart at people skills besides having the necessary technical skills for the job.

Eric M. Jackson of Canada-based Jackson Leadership Systems identified eight key attributes of smart leadership. They are: breeding "proactive paranoia"; "we work for the shareholders" mentality; the executive team and board have the answers, not the CEO; preventing groupthink; projecting authentic leadership; facing reality; desire to learn from mistakes; and, finally, personal accountability.

Smart leaders know their strengths and weaknesses thoroughly. They are a blend of both personal humility and professional will and are Level 5 Leaders in the language of Jim Collins. They continuously prepare themselves to shift from one effective zone to another when they find that the effective zone has become a comfort zone. They constantly rediscover and reinvent themselves with changing times and technologies. They are far ahead of their time. They love to live on the edge and prefer to be in the effective zone.

Smart leaders focus on people through soft leadership and on goals and objectives through hard leadership. They have smart work plans which are specific, measurable, achievable, realistic, and can be tracked. They are more of democratic leaders who consult others in decision-making and take their teams into confidence about the goals. They do not let a few people dominate the decision-making. They are aware that leadership is not just a matter of issuing commands, but involves leading by example and getting others to do what you want.

Smart Leadership = Soft + Hard Leadership

Smart leadership is all about making a balance between soft and hard power. Soft power is the art of getting the outcomes you want by attracting and persuading rather than by coercing and manipulating. In contrast, hard power depends on inducements by way of rewards or threats of punishment. It is more of a carrot-and-stick policy. Soft power believes in *win-win* while hard power follows *win-lose* policy.

It is often seen that military leaders believe in hard power while civilian leaders, especially the leaders in democratic countries, believe in soft power. Hitler demonstrated the power of hard leadership and Dalai Lama symbolizes soft leadership. What is required, in fact, is a blend of both soft and hard leadership, which is called smart leadership.

Businesses are changing rapidly and their needs have to be addressed through smart means and methods. As we are moving from market economy to network economy, there is a need for smart leadership that focuses both on soft and hard skills and makes a balance between both soft and hard power for handling the current complexities of the corporate world.

In the subsequent chapters, we will discuss in detail, with illustrations, examples, and case studies as to how to excel as smart leaders.

2

You Are the Leader!

"If you find a turtle on a fence post, it didn't get there by accident."
Calvin Coolidge

Everyone aspires for "success", but "success" itself is a relative term and there is no such thing in the world as absolute success. Success means different things to different people. For instance, success can mean achieving the impossible, making money, breaking records and getting recognized by others, coming out of comfort zone and entering into effective zone, getting up in the morning and doing what you want till you sleep, delivering your best unmindful of results, acquisition and application of knowledge, sharing knowledge and seeing others grow in front of you, achieving the desired outcomes, living in peace and harmony, giving back something to society, bridging the gap between aspirations and accomplishments, and so on. According to Emerson, success is "To laugh often and much; to win the respect of intelligent people and the affection of children; to earn the appreciation of honest critics and endure the betrayal of false friends; to appreciate beauty, to find the best in others; to leave the world a bit better, whether by a healthy child, a garden patch or a redeemed social condition; to know even one life has breathed easier because you lived." And Dr Joyce Brothers said, "Success is a state of mind. If you want success, start thinking of yourself as a success." Likewise, we find different definitions of success.

The process of achieving success can be defined as setting goals, working smart, persisting with efforts, managing external forces and factors, aligning yourself towards the goals, and, finally, accomplishing your goals. It involves unlocking and realizing your potential.

Achieving Success

Success comes from struggles and sacrifice. Success comes when you work hard, smart and wisely, while the rest of the world sleeps. Success comes when you take criticism constructively, learn your lessons, and move forward, rather than taking the criticism personally and getting dejected. Success comes when you are grateful for your blessings and are large hearted enough to work for making a difference to the lives of others.

Six Steps for Success

There are six steps for success: you must connect, communicate, understand, network, synergize, and accomplish the desired outcomes.

But first, you should have clarity of purpose. This is necessary for success.

You have a lot of strengths as an individual. It doesn't help anyone if your strengths lie hidden within yourself.

What you must do first is to connect with like-minded people to leverage your strengths to benefit yourself as well as others. This is the first step to success.

Next, you must communicate with others and build bridges with them, looking for similarities rather than differences. Communication conveys your strengths and weaknesses clearly to others, leading to mutual understanding and fraternity.

The third step is understanding. This ensures that other people respect your strengths and weaknesses. True understanding focuses on strengths and not weaknesses.

The fourth step to success is networking. This is a powerful tool in this globalized world. Several great people reached the pinnacle of success by the dint of their hard work, smart work, and network. We often hear the phrase, *"right person in the right place"*. This is applicable to people with hard work, smart work, and network. We also hear about *"the right person in the wrong place"*. This happens when people work hard and smart but don't have the necessary network. If a raindrop falls into a seashell it becomes a pearl, but if the same raindrop falls into an ocean, it gets merged with the water and loses its identity. Thus, networking is an amazing tool that catapults the right people to the right position, resulting in greater levels of success.

The fifth step to success is synergy. Stephen R. Covey said that synergy was one of the seven habits of highly effective people. Synergy is about leveraging the strengths of all the people in the group for achieving the best results. George Bernard Shaw once remarked, "If you have an apple and I have an apple and we exchange these apples then you and I will still have one apple each. But if you have an idea and I have an idea and we exchange these ideas, then each of us will have two ideas." In fact, the current world calls for more of collaboration than competition, as competition often creates ill will among people, while collaboration brings out the best from them and creates a *win-win* situation.

Finally, the sixth step to success is accomplishing the goals according to your expectations. This is the most crucial step as you face a number of challenges during execution. This step covers both internal and external factors or forces that will affect the accomplishment of the goals. When people don't accomplish their goals due to internal factors, they can diagnose the causes and take remedial measures. However, it is often seen that many people fail to achieve their goals due to external factors or forces beyond human control. The challenge, then, is to manage these factors or forces and still achieve success.

Thus, we can define the path to success as the six-step process of connecting, communicating, understanding, networking, synergizing and accomplishing the desired outcomes.

People must remember that success is only a means and not an end by itself. In fact, they should not run behind success. Unfortunately most of the people do so! It is better to work on the inborn talents first and then build skills and abilities around these talents. Often, people do the reverse by building their skills first and then aligning their talents with these skills. This is a retrograde process. When you adopt the right strategy along with the six-step process, success will run behind you.

Unlock the Genius within You

"Our deepest fear is not that we are inadequate. Our deepest fear is that we are powerful beyond imagination. It is our light more than our darkness which scares us. We ask ourselves–who are we to be brilliant, beautiful, talented, and fabulous? But honestly, who are you to not be so?" — Marianne Williamson

People often ignore their strengths due to their past failures, hurts, or external factors; have phobias and fears; and worry about success. The fact is that success does not come when you are unduly affected by past disappointments and setbacks. Success comes when you take action and move forward with optimism and confidence. Success comes when you blend both your hard and soft assets, where the hard assets are your skills, strengths, expertise, and experience, and soft assets are your passions, creative abilities, and values. Blending both hard and soft assets unlocks the genius within you.

Gina Rudan's *Practical Genius* unveils a five-step plan to "re-genius" you. These steps are: identify your genius, express your genius, surround yourself with genius, sustain your genius, and market your genius.

Tips to Unlock Your Genius

"Genius" is a relative term. Some people are "more genius" while some are "less genius". The truth is that the creative genius is lying deep inside each one of us and all we need to do is to find the key to unlock its potential. At the same time, remember not to compare yourself with others in terms of "level of genius". Here are some tips to unlock the genius, creativity, and potential within you.

- Visualize success. A battle is won twice—first in the mind and then in real life. Hence, when you believe that you have the potential, then it is easy to unlock the abilities and excel. It is rightly said, "if you think you can, you can; if you think you can't, you can't."
- Recognize and remove negative thoughts from your mind. They prevent you from absorbing positive thoughts and ideas. Research reveals that a person gets around 60,000 thoughts in a day and most of them are negative. Removing negative thoughts paves the way for attracting positive thoughts, leading to success.
- Focus on the present and let go the past. Studies reveal that people waste 30 percent of their precious time by thinking about the past that cannot be changed. Hence,

don't think too much about your unpleasant past, or about the future that cannot be predicted. Focus on the present to create your destiny. Be a warrior, not a worrier!

- Overcome your phobias and fears. Everyone has some kind of apprehensions which they may not reveal to others and most people think that they alone have such fears. Accept the fact that everyone has some apprehensions and try to overcome them.
- Avoid superstitions. At times superstitions stifle the creativity among the people, raising doubts about their competencies and capabilities, thus becoming obstacles to success.
- Avoid *fear of failure*. Dale Carnegie outlined the six kinds of fears people often have: fear of failure, fear of criticism, fear of old age, fear of poverty, fear of ill-health, and, finally, fear of death. Among all these fears, it is the fear of failure that prevents people from proceeding towards success. It is a fact that everyone fails at some point of time. This experience provides a number of lessons. To fail is not bad, but not to learn from the lessons is bad. Barack Obama remarked, "Making your mark on the world is hard. If it were easy, everybody would do it. But it's not. It takes patience, it takes commitment, and it comes with plenty of failure along the way. The real test is not whether you avoid this failure, because you won't. It's whether you let it harden or shame you into inaction, or whether you learn from it; whether you choose to persevere." Hence, avoid all kinds of fears so that you can unlock the genius and the potential within you.
- Solitude is fortitude. Go to a serene place, sit quietly for some time and don't let distractions divert your mind. Through meditation you can enjoy the power of calmness, peace, and tranquillity. Calmness and peace help in maximizing your potential.

- Avoid information overload. Studies reveal that, currently, the amount of information available gets doubled every year, unlike in 19th century when it took almost 100 years to double the available information. Pick up only what you need, as a lot of extraneous information is available on the internet. The extra information not only contaminates your mind but also wastes your time and stifles your creativity.

You Are the Leader!

Most people do not realize their real potential. They are under the impression that they don't have any creativity. The truth is that everyone has creativity and potential. But you have to take action to realize, recognize, and tap the hidden potential and creativity.

Creativity is like a sleeping elephant. The elephant has a huge potential, but it cannot see its own body because of its small eyes. The moment it realizes its potential, it can become the king of the jungle. In contrast, the lion knows its strengths and rules the jungle, although it is much smaller than the elephant in size. Similarly, you can be the king of your life once you recognize, realize, and unlock your potential.

In addition, potential is intangible and is infinite. The more you unlock it, the more you can exploit it and achieve your success. To conclude, unlock your hidden genius, blend both hard and soft assets and hard and soft skills, and follow the six -step process to achieve all round success to excel as a leader.

3

Leadership Lessons from Barack Obama

"Nothing can stop the man with the right mental attitude from achieving his goal; nothing on earth can help the man with the wrong mental attitude."
Thomas Jefferson

Operation Geronimo

Early morning on 2 May 2011, when the world was sleeping, two American helicopters with a 40-member US commando team, took off from the helipad base of Jalalabad in Afghanistan with a mission to free the world from its most wanted terrorist, Osama bin Laden. The mission had been planned much earlier by top CIA, anti-terrorist squad, and many intelligence agencies. The helicopters carrying the commandos, largely US Navy Seals famous for military acumen and excellence, reached the house in Abbottabad, Pakistan, where Osama was reported to have been hiding for the last five years. The commandos shot Osama dead and took away his body, while maintaining the safety of the civilians, and left the place safely. The entire operation lasted less than 40 minutes. It all happened like a Hollywood action film. The house in Abbottabad where Osama was shot dead was very close to Pakistan Military Academy and located 50 kilometres northeast of Islamabad, the capital of Pakistan.

The success of the operation was a result of the leadership qualities of Obama and coordination among the various intelligence agencies. It was also due to the commitment and team spirit of the commandos and US Navy Seals and, above all, the appropriate use of technology.

Pakistan was not informed in advance of the raid to ensure its successful execution.

Obama administration during Operation Geronimo

Obama vs. Osama

Although the names Obama and Osama appear to be similar, the personalities are poles apart. Barack Obama has a positive attitude and has grown as a successful global leader while Osama Bid Laden had a negative attitude and became a terrorist. Obama used his intelligence for the benefit of his country while Osama used it for destruction by unleashing terror. Osama's death is a lesson to all terrorists in the world. Those who live with violence die with violence and this is what happened to Osama.

Osama orchestrated the attacks on the twin towers of the World Trade Centre in New York and on the Pentagon on 11 September 2001. These attacks killed almost 3,000 people. Osama eluded capture for almost a decade. After his elimination Obama said, "This momentous achievement marks a victory for America, for people who seek peace around the world, and for all those who lost loved ones on September 11, 2001." And he declared, "Justice has been done."

Barack Obama

When compared with Jimmy Carter's Operation Eagle Claw to rescue American hostages in Iran, Obama's elimination of Osama was highly successful and without any casualties for American soldiers and civilians. When compared with the Bush administration, the Obama administration delivered better results in nailing Osama and tackling terrorism. Obama proved his political critics wrong by acting tough on global terrorism and being an assertive President. People have often mistaken Obama's velvet glove approach and gentle demeanour for weakness. They fail to recognize the toughness beneath his smile.

Leadership Lessons from Obama

Here are the leadership lessons from Obama:
1. **Don't drop a bomb when a slingshot can work.** Obama weighed all options before ordering the raid. He could have ordered bombing the compound, but he looked at the pros and cons and decided that a slingshot was enough to eliminate Osama. If the compound was bombed with an air strike and Osama was not in the compound at that time, it would become a huge diplomatic problem with Pakistan. Besides, it would be nearly impossible for America to confirm Osama's death in the rubble left behind after the air strike.
2. **Maintain neutral body language.** Obama maintains neutral body language and it is very tough for anyone to guess his thoughts from his body language. Operation Geronimo was planned three days earlier. Obama continued to perform all his usual activities normally, although he had this operation at the back of his mind. He did not reveal anything through his body language. He kept a poker face. The newspaper *Los Angeles Times* said, "All presidents keep secrets, but over a 72-hour span leading to Bin Laden's death, Obama's capacity to keep a poker face was tested as never before."
3. **Empower your team.** Obama empowers his team. He gave a free hand to the anti-terrorist team and other officials to make a plan to eliminate Osama. He did not interfere in their working. However, he did intervene and advise the team not to bomb the compound, as it was unwarranted and uncalled for. But most of the time Obama stayed away after empowering his team. The operation was planned by the anti-terrorist squad and the CIA, with a lot of coordination amongst themselves.
4. **Be assertive.** Obama is assertive by nature. Earlier, it was said that Obama was a weak President. But Obama proved his critics wrong by being assertive through this operation. Assertiveness is the art of saying *"No"*

firmly but politely. It is neither aggressiveness nor submissiveness and is the middle position between them. Assertiveness is about respecting one's rights without violating other people's rights. It emphasizes a win-win and a collaborative approach.

5. **Emphasize excellence, not perfection.** Excellence encourages risk taking while perfection is a phobia that discourages action. People who are more concerned about perfection do not take risks because they do not want to take a chance of making a mistake during execution. Obama believes in excellence, not perfection. Operation Geronimo was executed with excellence without any civilian casualties and achieved the desired result—elimination of Osama. However, the crash of a helicopter during the process is still a mystery, as reports reveal that it crashed after hitting the compound wall.

6. **Keep your mouth shut during execution.** Nothing was leaked although the plans had been made many days earlier. Obama opened his mouth only after the execution was complete and said, "We got him!"

7. **Give credit to your team.** After the operation was over, Obama thanked his team for the effective execution and did not stay in the limelight. He kept himself busy with other activities. He truly followed what Lao Tzu said, "A leader is best when people barely know that he exists; not so good when people obey and acclaim him; worst when they despise him. Fail to honour people, and they fail to honour you. But of a good leader, who talks little, when his work is done, his aim fulfilled, they will all say, 'We did this ourselves.'"

8. **Take calculated risks.** Obama knew the consequences of the failure of the military operation. The main challenge for him was to execute the operation in Pakistan, without informing the Pakistan government which had been its ally since long. He was caught between the devil and the deep blue sea. Finally, he accepted the advice of his

National Security Adviser, Thomas Donilon and his counter-terrorism adviser, John O. Brennan and took the decision to go ahead with the military operation.

9. **Don't trust even your old ally.** Obama had doubts in his mind about Pakistan, which had been sheltering Osama Bin Laden for a long time. But he did not reveal this in public. He maintained relations with Pakistan as earlier and, finally, surprised Pakistan by ordering the operation and thanking it for cooperation subsequently.

10. **Stay focused.** Obama means business. After he took over as the President, his priority was to make the US economy robust and to fight terrorism. He instructed CIA Chief Leon Panetta that either killing or capturing of Osama bin Laden was his top priority. He did not lose sight of his goals. Finally, Obama accomplished them.

11. **Be a Level 5 Leader.** Obama is a team player and a Level 5 Leader as described in Jim Collins book, *Good to Great*. He does not care who takes the credit for his achievements. The level 5 leaders are highly passionate and have professional will and personal humility. Obama stands out as a Level 5 Leader with great humility and thorough professional will.

The lessons from Obama's leadership are useful to all leaders, irrespective of their area of focus, whether it is politics, business, or military services.

Obama is a catalytic leader. He has the knack of managing a diverse group of people without hurting their egos and achieving the desired outcomes. He knows how to manage various egos, emotions, and feelings of his team members. He entered the White House when the US needed such a leader for turning around its economy and putting an end to global terrorism. He has been remarkably successful in both these areas.

4

Leadership is not a Popularity Contest

"Leadership is not popularity. It is getting results."

Peter Drucker

People often confuse leadership with popularity. In fact, leadership is more about taking responsibility and, as a result, inviting both bouquets and brickbats. It involves a lot of struggles and sacrifice. Leadership is often a thankless job as leaders are criticized for what was not done properly rather than appreciated for what was done well.

It is Lonely at the Top

It is true that it is lonely at the top, as leaders cannot discuss many things openly with others. They cannot associate freely with others in order to avoid controversies and getting involved in irrelevant issues. They cannot show their weaknesses to their peers and friends and have to be careful while talking to people to avoid being misunderstood. At times, associating with other people results in raising their expectations. The people then approach the leaders for favours which they may not be in a position to grant.

Popularity is a Bonus for Leaders

People often crave for success without realizing that success comes from regular commitment to excellence. When people strive for success rather than excellence, they may end up in failure as their main objective was incorrect. In contrast, when people are committed to excellence and work smart, they will be able to achieve their goals effectively. And in this journey to achieve excellence, if success comes, it becomes a bonus for them.

Similarly, those who want to lead must work without looking for popularity. When they do their best and deliver the results, popularity comes as a by-product. In contrast, if they look for popularity rather than leading effectively, they will end up in a disappointment. Hence, good leaders lay emphasis on the journey of commitment to excellence rather than on success and also on leading effectively rather than on popularity. None of the great leaders crave for popularity. They did what they felt was good for their people and acquired popularity as a bonus.

There are several challenges for leaders. They have to learn to handle praise as well as criticism, without being diverted from their goals. In addition, leaders cannot enjoy privacy and freedom like common persons. They cannot move freely for reasons of security. Overall, they have to struggle and sacrifice to be effective leaders.

Leaders take several decisions and all decisions may not bear the desired results. When some decisions go wrong, they are subjected to severe criticism and may even become unpopular. John Maxwell says, "The price of leadership is criticism. No one pays much attention to last place finishers, but when you're in front, everything gets noticed. Since leaders live with criticism it is important to learn to handle it constructively."

You cannot please all. You cannot be good to all. There is always a section of people who may not be happy with your leadership style, policies, or actions. Leaders like Mahatma Gandhi, Abraham Lincoln, John F. Kennedy, and Martin Luther King Jr, to name a few, were assassinated not because they were bad leaders but because they failed to please some people. Leaders can be good for some and bad for others. The fact is that a majority of the leaders want to do good things for their people. But when the interests of a particular section are affected, then the leaders are criticized and can even be assassinated.

Thus we have seen that leadership is not aimed at gaining popularity. Leadership is about taking responsibility and reaching the goals and objectives, unmindful of the bouquets and brickbats. It needs strong convictions and going ahead with the required actions even in the face of stiff opposition from a few quarters.

5

Be a Leader, Not a Boss

"People ask the difference between a leader and a boss. The leader works in the open, and the boss in covert. The leader leads, and the boss drives."
                                              Theodore Roosevelt

There is often confusion in differentiating between leaders and bosses. People use these terms synonymously, without appreciating the difference between the two. It is true that employees prefer to work with leaders rather than under bosses. We will discuss the differences between leaders and bosses in this chapter.

Bosses vs. Leaders

Bosses often speak as though they are omniscient. They have the attitude of *"I know everything"* and a huge ego. They have little respect for others and listen less and talk more. They have filters which block their minds and bias them with their preconceived notions and views. Sometimes bosses take the credit for the good work done by their subordinates and pass on the blame for the bad work done. However, leaders take the blame in case of failures and pass on the praise in case of successes.

Be a Leader, Not a Boss

Rajeev Peshawaria, in his book, *Too Many Bosses, Too Few Leaders: The Three Essential Principles You Need to Become an Extraordinary Leader* describes the difference between bosses and leaders. He talks about three parts of the organization—brains, bones and nerves, where brains are the setting of direction in the organization, bones are the execution, and nerves are the culture. Brains involve vision, strategy, and their widespread understanding, as well as unique capabilities. Bones are the process, structure, quality of talent, resource allocation, etc., and nerves are the leadership quality, short or long term focus, learning, and renewal. All these three are important for organizational effectiveness and excellence. Good leaders focus their time on developing them.

A boss exhibits a transactional attitude, while a leader displays a transformational attitude. A boss thinks that he knows everything, while a leader says he has to learn a lot more. A boss orders, while a leader directs. A boss demands respect, while a leader commands respect. A boss gets the job done, while the leader handholds others to do the job.

Russell H. Ewing differentiated between the two and said, "A boss creates fear, a leader confidence. A boss fixes blame, a leader corrects mistakes. A boss knows all, a leader asks questions. A boss makes work drudgery, a leader makes it interesting." Here are some differences between a boss and a leader.

1. The boss drives people; the leader coaches them.
2. The boss depends upon authority; the leader on goodwill.
3. The boss inspires fear; the leader inspires enthusiasm.
4. The boss says "I"; the leader says "We".
5. The boss says "Get here on time"; the leader gets there ahead of time.
6. The boss fixes the blame for the breakdown; the leader fixes the breakdown.

7. The boss knows how it is done; the leader shows how to do it.
8. The boss makes work tedious; the leader makes work fun.
9. The boss says "Go"; the leader says "Let's go".
10. The boss justifies or lays blame; the leader takes responsibility.

Transforming Bosses into Leaders

Leaders' role is to get the job done by others smoothly and successfully. When leaders are too conscious about their positions or if they become too proud, they become bosses. When excessive ego creeps into leaders, they behave like super heroes and neglect the egos, emotions, and feelings of others, and start behaving as bosses.

The members of the group feel uncomfortable with such bosses. If there is an option, people leave the organizations which have such bosses and if there is no option, they are forced to work under pressure from such bosses.

This is the start of organizational politics. People group together and play petty politics. They try to throw out these bosses to ensure their own survival. Hence, acting as a boss is not peaceful either for the person or for the people around him.

Sometimes it may also happen that bosses themselves don't know how to behave like leaders. In such cases, receiving 360 degree feedback can help them know where they stand so that they can transform and reinvent themselves. Leadership training programmes can also help.

Those who hold senior positions must remember that it is the referent power that carries more strength than positional or legitimate power. Such realization and awareness can transform bosses into leaders. When asked what his secret was for lasting so long and being so successful as the president of Yale University, Dr James R. Angell explained, "Grow antennae, not horns."

Hence, be a leader, not a boss.

6

Articulate Your Vision Effectively

"There's nothing more demoralizing than a leader who can't clearly articulate why we're doing what we're doing."

James Kouzes and Barry Posner

Leaders must know how to construct and articulate their vision effectively. There are leaders who have great imagination, intelligence, expertise, and communication abilities, but do not have clarity of vision, resulting in their eventual failure. In this chapter we will discuss about vision, the relation between vision and leadership and, above all, about visionary leaders.

Vision and Mission

Vision should not be confused with a dream. Vision is, in fact, a reality that is yet to occur. You will find many organizations having a vision and mission statement. Vision describes *where* the organization is expected to reach and mission describes *how* the organization is expected reach there. Setting, constructing, and articulating its vision helps the organization to achieve success as the managers can constantly align their goals and objectives with the organization's vision and modify their actions accordingly.

Importance of Vision

The English essayist James Allen wrote, "You will become as great as your dominant aspiration.... If you cherish a vision, a lofty ideal in your heart, you will realize it." It is the vision that keeps you moving forward with energy and enthusiasm. It is the vision that won't let you sleep and motivates you to work hard.

Vision helps you to align your team and give them specific roles and responsibilities. Vision helps in setting goals. It keeps your people focused on the goals and objectives.

Vision connects the present to the future, with a commitment to achieve the goals. It connects the present realities to the future aspirations. It brings people together because of the shared values and common goals. It enhances commitment and helps the team to stay focused.

Rosabeth Moss Kanter remarked, "A vision is not just a picture of what could be; it is an appeal to our better selves, a call to become something more." People must have at least a broad vision about where they want to go. Leaders must possess a vision which is far beyond the thinking of an average individual. The vision of leaders should start where the vision of the average person ends. It is the vision that differentiates between followers and leaders. Leaders think of the *where* and *why* while doing things, while the followers think of *how* and *when*. Having a vision which is not accompanied by action will make it a fantasy or a daydream. At the same time, action which is not preceded by vision may end up in a nightmare.

It is essential to communicate the vision. Leaders should have the ability to articulate their vision effectively to enable their followers know where they are headed. Only when the vision is clear to them, will the followers be able to go ahead with conviction.

Leaders and Vision

"The very essence of leadership is that you have to have a vision. It's got to be a vision you articulate clearly and forcefully on every occasion." — Theodore Hesburgh, President of the University of Notre Dame

The former President of America, John F. Kennedy had a vision to put an American astronaut on the moon and inspired Americans to commit firmly to his vision. He said, "I believe that this nation should commit itself to achieving the goal, before this decade is out, of landing a man on the Moon and returning him safely to the Earth." He effectively articulated his vision and worked towards realizing the goals.

Besides knowing how to articulate their vision to the people to achieve the desired objectives, leaders should write down their vision, so that the people understand it clearly and, eventually, achieve it.

Dr Martin Luther King Jr was a Civil Rights leader who effectively articulated his vision through his famous speech, "I have a Dream". He could convince and galvanize Americans to support the Civil Rights movement. He was a transformational leader who transformed the American society through non-violent and peaceful methods of Mahatma Gandhi. Similarly, Eleanor Roosevelt envisioned a world of equal opportunities for women and minorities.

Some leaders are reluctant to communicate their vision as they fear that not accomplishing it would mean the loss of their position. However, this creates doubts among their followers. When vision is set properly, the chances of achieving it are higher because it provides guidelines and road map for people to proceed. People have better clarity about themselves and their organization. Not to have a vision is like walking blind. Helen Keller rightly said, "The most pathetic person in the world is someone who has sight, but has no vision."

How to Craft a Vision

Peter Drucker said that the best way to predict the future is to create it. Your destiny is in your hands if you craft a suitable vision and articulate it effectively.

Crafting a vision involves a lot of effort. It involves attentive listening and information gathering. The vision must include the values and principles of the leader. Once a vision is crafted, half of the job is done. The other half of the job is to articulate the vision effectively. You may have numerous ideas and insights. But these are of consequence only when people know what they are, which is possible only when they are communicated effectively.

When you determine your vision, you must be clear about your goals. The goals must be SMART — **S**pecific, **M**easurable, **A**chievable, **R**eachable, and **T**rackable. Your goals must be ambitious and should motivate your people to move forward with a firm commitment to achieve them. The goals must be simple and straightforward, must be challenging and compelling, must be future oriented, and must align with the organizational objectives, principles, philosophies, and values.

Determining the vision alone is not enough, articulating it is equally important so that it is established effectively not just in the minds of the followers, but also in their hearts. Many leaders with extraordinary intelligence and imagination failed due to their inability to effectively articulate their ideas and insights.

Leaders who are good at articulating their vision clearly win the confidence, love, and affection of their followers. Articulation helps in accomplishment of vision as it increases understanding and helps to enhance commitment and clarity among the followers. Be it the Martin Luther King Jr, John F. Kennedy, Mahatma Gandhi or any other leader, their effective articulation of their visions paved the way for their successful achievement.

Visionary Leaders

Peter Kreeft, a professor of philosophy at Boston College, says, "To be a leader you have to lead people to a goal worth having—something that's really good and really there."

Visionary leaders have the art of telling stories to communicate and connect with their people. Steve Jobs was an amazing example. He took Apple to great heights through his creativity, innovation and imagination. Warren Buffet is a visionary leader who has a great ability to figure out where the markets will head in future. This has made him one of the most successful investors in the world. Both Steve Jobs and Warren Buffett became visionary leaders as they saw beyond what is usually seen by others. They have more of conceptual skills and see the big picture better than others.

My Personal Journey

"The future belongs to those who see possibilities before they become obvious." —John Scully

I have a vision to become one of the top leadership gurus in the world. But how can I achieve it? Should I simply set a vision and sleep over it without any action? No. I have done extensive research about where I want to reach in life and how I can excel as a leadership guru. After the research, it was clear that I had to have an international presence, which takes a lot of time. Hence, I decided to contribute articles in the area of leadership and started posting my blogs titled "Where Knowledge is Wealth" at http://profmsr.blogspot.com and "Knowledge Grows When Shared" at http://professormsraoguru.blogspot.com.

Initially, nobody took the blogs seriously. But, gradually, as the posts increased, there were more visitors to my blogs. I now have several followers who regularly read my blogs the way they read their newspapers every day. And if I don't post for more than a week, I get mails in my inbox enquiring if I was unwell and asking reasons for not posting articles. In addition, many visitors post their comments, thus adding value to my blogs. Other leadership gurus have also started visiting my blogs. I also began getting assignments for training programmes. I conducted several training programmes on leadership and shared my knowledge with the participants.

At the same time, I began doing research in the area of leadership. I found that there were two million definitions of leadership and there were half a billion hits on the terms *leaders* and *leadership*. This showed the interest these terms are creating globally and the potential in the domain of leadership.

Since the domain was already crowded, in order to differentiate myself, I decided to follow the road less travelled. I did some intensive research and found some gaps in our understanding of what kind of leadership is needed in the current context and in the current world. Then I started focusing on soft leadership and authored a book on it. The book received endorsements from top global leadership gurus, who were already reading my blogs and were impressed with them and by my passion in the area of leadership.

Apart from soft leadership, I also authored several books on leadership and success. The sales of these books picked up gradually, making a name for me as an author. I also began writing articles on leadership. After a lot of rejections, many international journals and magazines accepted my articles for publications and, finally, I was invited to join a few prestigious publications as an Editorial Board Member and reviewer.

I received invitations from many educational institutions and companies to share my knowledge on leadership. This provided me an opportunity to establish myself gradually as an expert on leadership. When I interacted with industry experts and bright students, they asked many questions on leadership that provided new triggers to my thoughts. I researched on these ideas and found answers which added value to my existing knowledge. Over a period of time, I acquired more competency in the domain and became more comfortable as I overcame my weaknesses. I always took feedback seriously. This helped me to evolve as a leadership expert.

I began networking with other leadership gurus who accepted me wholeheartedly and communicated with me through emails. I strongly believe in collaboration rather than competition. My strategy of putting in hard work, smart work, wise work, and network helped me to grow gradually as an international leadership expert. Above all, I followed the path less travelled.

From my biography it is very clear that success does not come overnight. We need to work with a compelling vision with effective execution and feedback. However, I was willing to wait patiently and was continuously learning and growing in my domain. I strongly believed in my dreams and vision. I did not change my goal but only changed my strategies to reach the goal of becoming a global leadership guru.

When you look at leaders like John F. Kennedy, Mahatma Gandhi, Martin Luther King Jr, Aung San Suu Kyi, Bob Hawke, and Sir Richard Branson, it is obvious that they are all visionary leaders who are blessed with the gift of communication and can craft and articulate their vision effectively. It is their articulation of vision that sets them apart from other leaders. There is a Japanese proverb, "Vision without action is a daydream and action without vision is a nightmare". Both vision and execution are essential for achieving the desired results.

7

Follow the Road Less Travelled

"Two roads diverged in a wood and I–I took the one less traveled by."
Robert Frost

Leaders must learn to follow the road less travelled to stay ahead of others. This is the age of uncertainty and complexity where things are changing rapidly. The leaders must constantly innovate and find out new ways and means to take their organizations to greater heights of success. In this chapter we will discuss about Steve Jobs who followed the road less travelled and made all the difference to Apple Computers.

Steve Jobs—Innovative Leader

"Innovation has nothing to do with how many R&D dollars you have. When Apple came up with the Mac, IBM was spending at least 100 times more on R&D. It's not about money. It's about the people you have, how you're led, and how much you get it." — Steve Jobs

Steve Jobs was one of the iconic CEOs of the world and was a leader who always set high standards in innovation.

He changed the way people use technology. Apple's success can be ascribed to two things—visionary leadership and innovative leadership. Steve Jobs was a rare leader who possessed both these leadership traits and integrated them effectively to make Apple a global leader.

Steve Jobs

In fact, Steve Jobs was synonymous with Apple. Nobody expected that this college dropout would create history in the business world. But he did, through his unconventional strategies, unflagging determination, and perseverance. Nobody expected that the man who was fired from his job as a CEO would return and be in command for 14 years at a stretch and take his organization to such great success. It is often said that the people who are fired from jobs lose their morale, energy, and enthusiasm. In contrast, Steve Jobs persisted, returned, and turned around the company which was then on the brink of disaster.

Steve Jobs was a college dropout like some other famous corporate leaders—Richard Branson, Bill Gates, Larry Ellison, Michael Dell, and Mark Zuckerberg. He rose from humble origins and was a symbol of hard work and hope for millions of people across the world.

If you ask any child what the alphabet "A" stands for, the response will be, "A is for Apple". If you ask the same question to an American child, the response would be "A is for Apple and innovation." This is the image Apple created in America and across the world under the leadership of Steve Jobs. Apple has created new products and services by following the road less travelled. It took many years for Apple to build a name for innovation. Here are the lessons you can learn from the leadership provided by Steve Jobs:

Follow Your Passion

Follow your passion, as your passion will ultimately deliver the goods and determine your destiny. It is a fact that the people who pursue their passions rather than money earn both name and fame and carve a niche for themselves. The success of iPod was due to the fact that Steve Jobs passionately spent four hours a week, 50 weeks a year, for 12 years, discussing with software, hardware, and design experts to produce the best ideas for the product.

When you work in areas where you have a passion, you enjoy your life and provide a meaning to your life. Over a period of time you will be contributing your best, thus delivering amazing outcomes. When people work in domains where they have a passion, they don't get stressed due to their deep involvement and commitment. Such people create their own identity and build their own image. In the long run, they are recognized and rewarded. And money starts flowing in eventually. In contrast, when people work for money, they ruin their health as they don't enjoy their work and, ultimately, spend whatever they have earned on doctors and medicines. Wayne Dyer, author and speaker said, "When I chased after money, I never had enough. When I got my life on purpose and focused on giving of myself and everything that arrived into my life, then I was prosperous."

Be a Visionary

Steve Jobs was a great visionary. Where the imagination of others stopped, his imagination began and that made him stand out. He had clarity of vision. He knew where he wanted to go and how he would take his people there. He created visual images and used them to connect with his people effectively. He was a great speaker who communicated well and articulated his vision effectively to his people. Only when vision is strong and well articulated can leaders expect to accomplish their goals.

Be Focused

Steve Jobs was clearly focused on his goals and objectives. He worked throughout his life with passion and dedication to achieve his goals. He said, "People think focus means saying yes to the thing you've got to focus on. But that's not what it means at all. It means saying no to the hundred other good ideas that there are. You have to pick carefully."

Be a Team Builder

Steve Jobs was very selective in choosing the right talent. He had the knack of hiring the right people with right attitude and had tremendous ability to build teams and capitalize on their strengths. He noted, "My job is to not be easy on people. My job is to make them better. My job is to pull things together from different parts of the company and clear the ways and get the resources for the key projects. And to take these great people we have and to push them and make them even better, coming up with more aggressive visions of how it could be."

Set an Example

Leaders can influence others only by setting an example. Steve Jobs dedicated his life to technology. He delivered his best and expected the best from others. This had tremendous impact on others and they contributed their best for achieving organizational effectiveness and excellence.

Have Tenacity

Steve Jobs was famous for his tenacity and resilience. He was an adopted child. In his younger days he survived by selling Coke bottles and having free meals at the Hare Krishna temple in Oregon. He did not lose heart when he was fired from the job of the CEO of the company he founded.

About his ouster from Apple, he said, "It was awful-tasting medicine, but I guess the patient needed it. Sometimes life's gonna hit you in the head with a brick. Don't lose faith." Instead of blaming his circumstances, he focused on his work. He pursued his passion for technology.

When he was recalled to Apple a few years later, many doubted his capabilities in the prevailing business environment. He proved his critics wrong and put Apple on the top through his passion and perseverance. He displayed tremendous tenacity and fought against all the odds stacked against him.

Be Persistent

Thomas Alva Edison failed a number of times to invent the light bulb. When asked about it, he said that he did not fail, but learnt a number of ways that did not work. It is persistence that makes people achieve big things. Steve Jobs was persistent. He failed a number of times in his professional life. Each time he learnt his lessons and moved on, without having any regrets. He once remarked, "I'm convinced that about half of what separates the successful entrepreneurs from the non-successful ones is pure perseverance."

Strive for Excellence

Aristotle said, "Men acquire a particular quality by constantly acting in a particular way." Steve Jobs acquired the quality of excellence by constantly working on technology. He emphasized on value addition to the existing products and services through constant innovation and creativity. He believed in excellence rather than perfection. He raised the bar for himself and for others. This ultimately led to excellence, thus getting ahead of competitors. He said, "Be a yardstick of quality. Some people aren't used to an environment where excellence is expected."

Build Your Brand

People find it tough to imagine Apple without Steve Jobs since he created a huge impact and impression on the minds of everyone. His successor Timothy Cook has a tough challenge ahead. Professor David B. Yoffie, Harvard Business School, expressed the same concern, "The real challenge for Apple will be what happens beyond that road map. Apple is going to need a new leader with a new way of recreating and managing the business in the future."

Whenever charismatic leaders leave, their successors feel the pressure of expectations. The new leaders find it difficult to meet the aspirations and expectations of the customers and other stakeholders. In the case of Timothy Cook, it will be more difficult as his predecessor, who was a charismatic leader and whose impact was deeply felt all over the world, has left a strong legacy. However, Timothy Cook's journey may be smooth, as Steve Jobs' departure, due to his poor health, was planned in advance and the succession plan was prepared much earlier.

When the legendary Jack Welch left General Electric, the scrip fell. His successor Jeff Immelt found it tough to match the charisma of his predecessor. However, through soft leadership, he could succeed in the challenging business environment. Similarly, Timothy Cook will evolve gradually as a leader with his own identity.

Steve Jobs falls into the category of hard leaders. Transactional leaders like Jack Welch manage business with a task orientation. Although hard leadership is not appreciated in the current management thought, it is still prevalent and we cannot totally get away from this style as leaders have different attitudes, aptitudes, styles, and temperaments. Steve Jobs becomes an interesting case study for many, be it students or executives. He proved that everything was possible in this world through passion, vision, mission, execution and, above all, innovation.

Most of the charismatic leaders leave a leadership vacuum when they leave. They make their absence felt more in their absence. Although Steve was a charismatic leader and planned his succession well, but still his absence will be felt.

Make Your Choices Wisely

Steve Jobs realized sometime in February 2011 that his time was near. Hence, he made his own choices and spent his last days wisely with his wife and four children, to avoid leaving any regrets at his death. He led a complete life. He gave sleepless nights to his competitors such as Microsoft and Google. Although Steve Jobs is no more, his ideas will be with us for many years.

Be an Icon

When the entire technological world got into the so called PC wars, Steve Jobs took the path less travelled and became a trailblazer and a legend. He started as a small fish in a big pond and ultimately became a big pond of innovation and excellence. He rewrote the rules of business and changed the way technology works. He made a big difference to the lives of people through his technological contributions. He will be remembered not only for his outstanding contributions, but also for his visionary and innovative leadership.

Expert vs. Referent Power

"Stars don't work for idiots." — John Sullivan, San Francisco State University

Leadership and power are closely connected as we saw in the case of Steve Jobs who wielded referent power. According to the social psychologists John French and Bertam Raven, power is divided into five forms—legitimate, coercive, reward, expert, and referent power. The power a person has because of the legal standing vested in him by the organization is known as legitimate power. Such people hold power as long as they hold their legitimate positions. Coercive power is a negative power which comes from threats or punishments that usually prevail in autocratic societies and people with such power are hardly respected. Reward power is the power exercised by those who have the ability to reward others. These people enjoy their power as long as they can give rewards to others. Expert power is the power of people who have expertise in some areas, for example the power of domain experts. Finally, referent power is the power leaders have not because of any law or position, but because people admire them as leaders. Leaders such as Mahatma Gandhi, Martin Luther King Jr, and Mother Teresa possessed referent power as people revered and support them. Although Steve Jobs started with strengths based on his domain expertise and innovation, he eventually had referent power. Most of the leaders survive on their expert power and fade away after some time. However, real leaders have referent power.

Steve Jobs—a Symbol of Iconic Leadership

Steve Jobs was a visionary leader, an inspirational leader and, above all, a charismatic leader. He kept Apple healthy and strong by keeping competitors at bay through his innovative and inspiring leadership. He was not only a great American leader but also a global leader who inspires all of us.

8

Emphasize "Means", not "Ends"

"There are seven things that will destroy us: Wealth without work; Pleasure without conscience; Knowledge without character; Religion without sacrifice; Politics without principle; Science without humanity; Business without ethics."

Mahatma Gandhi

Leaders must learn lessons from the collapse of several big companies due to the unethical practices and methods of their leaders. When leaders emphasize "ends" rather than "means", such downfalls happen. Hence, let us discuss about ethics, which is the key to the success and effectiveness of leadership.

When you evaluate the reasons for the collapse of companies such as Enron, Tyco, Lehman Brothers, WorldCom, and Global Crossing, it becomes clear that there was a complete disregard for ethics among their leaders. This is the reason why there is a need for teaching ethics in business schools. But, will teaching ethics alone suffice? The answer is clearly, "No!" Ethics is something that needs to be emphasized not only in business schools but also in corporate training to enable leaders to be aligned to ethical habits and practices.

What is Insider Trading?

Insider trading is a white collar crime. It is about trading of stocks on the basis of internal information which is not available to general public. Usually such information is known and accessible only to the senior managers within the company. Insider trading helps the traders to buy or sell the shares of the company at the right time, either to make money or to reduce losses. In this process, the ordinary investors lose money as they get the information much later. By then the manipulators have completed their transactions and are safe.

Leaders must realize that it is tough to climb the ladder of success, but very easy to fall from the top due to wrongdoing. When leaders emphasize on ends instead of means, they may end up in a great disaster. They should not get tempted by short term gains, which prove to be costly in the end. Here is a list of some leaders who fell from grace:

Jeff Skilling, the former CEO of Enron which went bankrupt due to an accounting scandal, was convicted in 2006 on one charge of insider trading and 18 counts of fraud and conspiracy. He was sentenced to 24 years in jail.

TV personality Martha Stewart was indicted for insider trading in 2003. Stewart saved over $45,000 by dumping her ImClone stock just before it dropped, using information from that company provided by an insider. She was jailed for five months.

Former IBM executive Robert Moffat gave inside information to New Castle Funds consultant Danielie Chiesi, who was one of the key people in Galleon's Raj Rajaratnam's network of people providing inside information. Moffat was sentenced to six months imprisonment and fined $ 50,000.

Tyco International Ltd.'s L. Dennis Kozlowski and WorldCom Inc.'s Bernie Ebbers were convicted for similar misdeeds.

Ethical Leadership

James MacGregor Burns said, "Divorced from ethics, leadership is reduced to management and politics to mere technique." Both ethics and leadership are closely connected for effectiveness of leadership. Ethics is something that should be cultivated among all people whether they are leaders or followers.

In order to make a beginning, the leaders have to take the responsibility to be ethical in their practices and influence others to do that same. Hence, there is a need for ethical leadership.

Ethics is all about emphasizing "means" rather than "ends". Ethics is all about values and morals. According to Albert Schweitzer, "Ethics is the activity of man directed to secure the inner perfection of his own personality." And Potter Stewart says, "Ethics is knowing the difference between what you have a right to do and what is right to do." Thus, we can define ethical leadership as one which leads from the front with moral values and principles and with an emphasis on means rather than ends.

Leaders are always closely observed. People search for negative things among the leaders rather than positive things. Hence, leaders have to be very careful all the time. They must display honesty, integrity, and total transparency in their dealings so that they influence others in a positive way.

People respect leaders more for their ethical values than any other traits such as charisma, compassion, or commitment. Although all these traits are needed for effective leadership, it is ethics that differentiates the leaders. It is rightly said that although the righteous person falls ten times, he rises if his means are right as God supports him.

However, the person, who does wrong and who emphasizes on ends, never falls twice as there is no second opportunity for him.

Ethical Leaders

"I am not interested in power for power's sake, but I'm interested in power that is moral, that is right and that is good." — Martin Luther King, Jr

Leaders like Martin Luther King Jr, Mahatma Gandhi, Mother Teresa, and Dalai Lama have emphasized more on means, although ends are also important. It is their emphasis on means and methods which brought them laurels and made them legends. If Martin Luther King Jr had adopted violent means to bring blacks on par with whites, would he have become a great leader? If Mahatma Gandhi had adopted violent means to attain India's independence, would he have lived as a great leader in the hearts of the people for so long a time? No, never!

Mother Teresa lived for the poor and the lepers and made a significant difference to their lives. Although Florence Nightingale was a rich woman, she gave up her comforts to serve patients in the Crimean war. Presently, the Dalai Lama is seeking Tibet's independence through non-violent means. Aung San Suu Kyi fought for democracy in Burma through peaceful means. All these leaders stood out basically because they emphasized more on "means" than on "ends".

In contrast, Hitler used wrong means to achieve his ends. Although Hitler was a capable leader who emphasized on German pride, he persecuted Jews and put them into concentration camps.

There were several leaders who misused their powers, either to misguide their people or to serve their own selfish interests. Such leaders were soon forgotten. Hence, what counts at the end of the day are the ethics and values.

J. R. D. Tata—An Ethical Business Leader

"Though negotiations are a rough game, you should never allow them to become a dirty game. Once you've agreed to a deal, don't back out of it unless the other party fails to deliver as promised. Your handshake is your bond. As far as I'm concerned, a handshake is worth more than a signed contract. As an entrepreneur, a reputation for integrity is your most valuable commodity. If you try to put something over on someone, it will come back to haunt you." — Victor Kiam

J. R. D. Tata of the Tata Group was a symbol of ethical leadership. He emphasized "means" rather than "ends". This helped the group to survive much turbulence. At the same time, adhering to ethical values slowed the pace of growth, paving the way for the emergence of other business houses. But he did not regret this. He said, "I have often thought about that. If we had done some of the things that some other groups have done, we would have been twice as big as we are today. But we did not, and I would not have it any other way."

Following his footsteps, Ratan Tata maintained the same standards. He preferred to exit unfair business transactions than compromise on his values. He said, "I would hope that my successors would never compromise and turn to soft options to meet their ends."

It is true that all effective leaders may not be ethical leaders, but all ethical leaders can be effective leaders as they influence others through their own example. Nothing is more powerful than setting example while leading others.

To conclude, no organization can survive without ethics, rules and regulations, policies and procedures, and a vision and a mission. However, some companies resort to "short cuts". In a hurry to reach to the top and to beat competition, they compromise on ethics. In the end, they have to pay a heavy price when the truth comes out. Similarly, leaders who adopt unethical means end up losing whatever they earned. Hence, emphasize more on "means" rather than "ends". A life spent in simplicity and humility is far better than a life spent with fame initially and infamy finally.

9

Manage Uncertainty

"Without the element of uncertainty, the bringing off of even the greatest business triumph would be dull, routine, and eminently unsatisfying."

J. Paul Getty

When Alexander the Great was passing through the Gedrosian desert with an army of 30,000 soldiers and cavalry units, he suddenly found himself in a crisis when they lost their way. It was the peak of summer and the soldiers were thirsty due to the scorching heat. But Alexander gave no sign of panic. He remained cool, calm, and composed. He asked the local guides, but they did not know the way. Alexander, with a few soldiers, searched for the right route by moving in different directions. By sheer luck they finally caught sight of the blue sea from a low rise in the dunes. He ordered the rest of the army to move forward in the correct direction and saved his men from potential disaster. In this case Alexander managed uncertainty through intuition, which comes from experience and intelligence.

There is often a wide gap between vision and execution. Although leaders work hard and create a smart vision and try to pursue it through effective execution, they find that invariably some unforeseen events add to the uncertainty of the outcomes. In this chapter we will discuss about uncertainty which has become the hallmark of the 21st century.

We always need to anticipate the external challenges that may arise in the future and work accordingly. Most of the times what we plan does not happen and we must be ready to deal with such situations and take actions accordingly. We must remove misalignments on the way, make corrections, and move forward.

The biggest challenge for leaders in the 21st century is how to manage change. Constant change leads to uncertainty. We all know that change is the only constant in this world, but it is difficult to predict the direction in which change will take place.

Uncertainty Everywhere

Uncertainty is everywhere in the world. Whether it is leaders or followers, employers or employees, rich or poor, everybody is subjected to uncertainty. Since uncertainty cannot be avoided, people must learn to cope with it by preparing themselves mentally. They must cultivate a mindset which looks for opportunities in uncertainties and build an attitude of optimism and confidence. Only then they will be able to survive in this world. Ram Charan in his book, *Leadership in the Era of Economic Uncertainty: The New Rules for Getting the Right Things Done in Difficult Times* discusses uncertainty, especially in the context of recession.

How to Manage Uncertainty?

Whenever we are confronted with uncertainty, we have to identify the issues that create challenges for us. We need to look at the impact or damage to our plans or the tasks. We need to find the root cause of the problems and work out feasible solutions which will keep us aligned to our goals. We must take remedial actions and then monitor them closely to determine if we have succeeded in resolving the problem.

Leaders at All Levels

Leaders are aware that uncertainty is everywhere and they must embrace it to make things happen. They must also make others realize this fact and make it a part of operating reality.

There are three ways to take decisions. When leaders take a decision with adequate information it is known as certainty. When leaders take a decision with inadequate information it is known as risk. When leaders take a decision with little or variable information it is known as uncertainty. Leaders at lower levels of management take decisions with adequate information, leaders at middle levels of management take decisions with inadequate information and leaders at higher level management take decisions with little or uncertain information.

It is clear that leaders take decisions at every level of management, but their decision making depends on availability of inputs and, at times, unavailability of inputs. It may appear strange how the leaders at top levels of management can take decisions without complete information! When leaders reach the top position, they possess more of conceptual skills and less of technical skills and this helps them to take decisions with few inputs and manage uncertainty.

Uncertainty is not always unhealthy. It can lead to creativity and innovation if people think out of the box and come out with new solutions and ideas. R. I. Fitzhenry remarked, "Uncertainty and mystery are energies of life. Don't let them scare you unduly, for they keep boredom at bay and spark creativity." Hence, uncertainty can be good for people. It keeps them on their toes and keeps them alert all the time.

In these times of increased uncertainty, making Plan A and Plan B is not enough. Leaders must prepare Plan C also to manage the complexity and uncertainty, as things often do not work out as planned and scheduled.

To conclude in the words of Erich Fromm, "The quest for certainty blocks the search for meaning. Uncertainty is the very condition to impel man to unfold his powers."

10

Stay Calm in the Eye of the Storm

"Be like a duck. Calm on the surface, but always paddling like the dickens underneath."

Michael Caine

When you look at leaders like Winston Churchill, Abraham Lincoln, Boris Yeltsin, and Rudy Giuliani, the common thread connecting them is that they led with a cool and calm demeanour and handled crises effectively. Winston Churchill was a war time hero who led his country to victory during the Second World War. Abraham Lincoln was the President at a crucial time in American history, when he had to work for the unity of the country and also against slavery at the same time. Boris Yeltsin handled an army coup successfully by facing it head-on. Rudy Giuliani, as the Mayor of New York, handled the aftermath of the 9/11 attacks. These leaders remained calm during the crisis and set an example for others to follow. They were cool, composed, and charismatic in their leadership. In this chapter we will discuss about the leaders and entrepreneurs who acted similarly.

Calm Leadership

Leaders must lead from the front during a crisis. They must be visible to the people and build confidence among them that they are with them. In fact, a crisis reveals the true colours and real skills of leaders. Winston Churchill demonstrated his leadership skills during the war. However, he failed during peace time, which shows that some leaders perform better during stress and crises than under normal conditions.

Calm leaders focus on managing the available resources instead of blaming the external circumstances. They have the ability to handle complexity and uncertainty and yet remain calm. For instance, before the execution of Operation Geronimo, Obama maintained neutral body language and kept a cool demeanour although the operation was planned much earlier. During all this time, he performed his usual duties in a normal manner.

Leaders must remain calm while being at the centre of the storm. When everything goes awry, they must demonstrate a cool composure and work out strategies to manage and lead their team. They should send strong signals to their subordinates to maintain their trust and confidence. Calm leaders let go of things they have no control of and focus on what they can actually control. For instance, the current global economic crisis needs some degree of calmness and some degree of action. The calm leaders focus on action rather than getting overly anxious about economic factors that are beyond their control.

Crisis is an Opportunity, not a Threat

Publilius Syrus once said, "Anyone can hold the helm when the sea is calm." The real leaders emerge during a storm. And real leadership skills emerge during a crisis. The leaders who fail to rise to the occasion during a crisis will never succeed as leaders. In fact, a crisis is not a threat but an opportunity to test you and to enable you to help others to make a difference through performance.

Entrepreneurs Remain Calm

Albert Einstein said, "In the middle of difficulty lies opportunity." Similarly, entrepreneurs have the ability to spot opportunities within threats. For instance, when the Mexican economy was in ruins in 1982, Carlos Slim saw the opportunities and invested heavily during the downturn. When everybody believed there was a catastrophe, Carlos seized the opportunities available and today he is one of the richest persons in the world. Similarly, Amadeo P. Giannini, who founded the San Francisco-based Bank of Italy, which was later renamed as Bank of America, also converted threats into opportunities

It is a fact that unintended consequences ignite unexpected opportunities and entrepreneurs take advantage of such opportunities. From the examples of Carlos Slim and Amadeo P. Giannini, it is clear that they remained calm and collected during crises, converted threats into opportunities, and became successful. Hence, leaders have to remain calm in the eye of the storm.

We will now discuss how Abraham Lincoln, Boris Yeltsin, and Rudolph W. Giuliani handled huge crises effectively.

Lincoln's Leadership

During the American Civil War, several states seceded from the American Union and formed the Confederacy. On December 20, 1860, South Carolina, followed within two months by Mississippi, Florida, Alabama, Georgia, Louisiana, and Texas, seceded from the Union. By April 17, 1861, Virginia, Arkansas, Tennessee, and North Carolina also seceded from the Union, forming an eleven state Confederacy with a population of nine million, including nearly four million slaves.

There was a bitter battle between the forces of Confederacy and the American Union for supremacy. Abraham Lincoln was at the helm of affairs as the President of the American

Union. He had won with 40 per cent of popular votes, but found it tough to handle the situation. However, he remained calm and led the Union to victory, thus maintaining the integrity of America, and abolishing slavery. He proved to be one of the best American presidents and a role model for future presidents who, whenever faced with challenges, looked at learnings from Lincoln's leadership for guidance.

Boris Yeltsin

Russia's first freely elected president, Boris Yeltsin was a calm leader who led from the front and oversaw the transition of USSR to Russia. He had the courage to stand up to a military coup aimed at restoring a dictatorial regime in Russia.

Highlighting his achievements, *The Financial Times* commented, "Boris Yeltsin had the physical and moral strength to bear on his shoulders the colossal burden of a country in a ferment of transition, its economy struggling with the twin tasks of discarding a tenacious old system and adjusting to an unfamiliarly fast-moving new one. At the beginning of his rule he was able to grasp, either instinctively or through a quick intelligence, much of what was required."

Rudolph W. Giuliani

"When you confront a problem you begin to solve it."
—Rudolph W. Giuliani

Rudolph W. Giuliani was the Mayor of New York from 1994 to 2002. He displayed his amazing leadership skills during the September 11, 2001 terrorist attacks on New York. At that time his popularity was on the wane and it was believed that he would fade away into obscurity. But the terrorist attacks on the twin towers of the World Trade Centre brought his inner strength, potential, and character to the fore. Through his calm leadership, he brought remarkable strength and stability to New York when the city was clouded with uncertainty. He faced the crisis squarely, without losing his calm, led from the front, and consoled and reassured the public by building confidence in them. He said, "It is in times of crisis that good leaders emerge."

Giuliani outlines six skills to excel as a great leader. These are—having strong beliefs, being an optimist, being courageous, preparing relentlessly, emphasizing teamwork, and communicating clearly. *Time* magazine honoured him as the *Person of the Year* in 2001 and Queen Elizabeth II bestowed on him an honorary Knight Commander of the Most Excellent Order of the British Empire.

Leaders must be prepared to face any crisis that may occur, whether in the shape of a terrorist attack, natural calamity, negligence within the system, or industrial accidents. Failure to control the crisis quickly may damage the organization's credibility and goodwill.

Whenever you are confronted with a crisis, be a part of the solution, not a part of the problem. Of course, this is always very hard to remember in the heat of the moment! When hit with a sudden crisis, take a deep breath, look at the problem in detail, focus on the big picture, search for alternate solutions, shortlist the best one, and implement and execute effectively. Do remember that all actions may not deliver the desired outcomes. Be prepared for failures. When you act in a calm manner, you will find a solution to your problems. At the same time, prepare not just Plan A and Plan B, but also Plan C, and so on, to manage the uncertainty.

It is true that some leaders deliver well during stress and crisis as adversity brings out the best in them. When stress delivers positive results it is known as *eustress*. Vannevar Bush once said, "Fear cannot be banished, but it can be calm and without panic; it can be mitigated by reason and evaluation."

Leaders must control their emotions of anger and frustration and remain calm under pressure. It is essential for them to be seen as problem solvers in times of crisis rather than people who just complain. Staying calm during a storm will help you to come out with flying colours.

11

Use Your Time Effectively

"Time is an inelastic resource. No matter how high the demand, we cannot rent, hire or buy more of it."

Peter Drucker

Many companies conduct time management workshops for their employees to help them to learn how to manage their time efficiently. Such workshops enhance their productivity and performance at the workplace. At the same time, leaders must also be able to plan, prioritize, and manage their time judiciously. As people reach higher positions, their roles become more challenging. They need to be able to differentiate between what is important and what is unimportant and also what is urgent and what is not. We will discuss time management in this chapter as it is important for leaders to manage and get the most not only out of their own time, but from the time of their employees also.

Time management is more about using time judiciously rather than managing time. We all have only 24 hours in a day. We have only one life, and that too is full of complexity and uncertainty. Hence, we must identify our priorities and plan to achieve the desired goals on time. People often waste their time due to phobias and unreasonable fears which discourage them from pursuing their goals. But before we discuss using time efficiently, it is essential to spot the time wasters.

Spot Time Wasters

To track time wasters, note down how you spend your time every day for a week. At the end of the week check where you spent your time unnecessarily. For instance, if there was wastage of time in attending to unsolicited calls, then take actions to avoid them. If you find that you spent a lot of your time browsing the internet, then control it. If you find that visitors took too much of your time, then attend only to visitors who come with appointments. In a similar manner, you must find all the areas where you waste your time and then take actions to enable you to plan, prioritize, and manage your time.

Manage Your Mental Time

There is a correlation between your thoughts, mental conversations, and actions. Your thoughts will reflect your actions. Don't waste your time thinking about the events of your past which were not pleasant and which cannot be changed now. Studies reveal that people waste 30 per cent of their time by thinking about such events. Avoid worrying about your future either, as you cannot predict it. Instead, focus on the present on which you have control.

In addition, use your inner dialogue effectively. We all have inner dialogue where we talk to ourselves throughout our waking hours. We must learn to use that time productively and minimize wastage. This is your mental time management.

It is said that success starts from your mind. Similarly, you think within your mind first and then take action. Therefore, make use of your mental time effectively by using efficient time management tools so that you can manage your time better. This is a wonderful technique to save and manage your time.

Prepare a "To-Do" List

One of the best ways to manage time is to prepare a "to-do" list as it helps you to organize, prioritize, schedule, and act accordingly. But this requires that you first spend your time in meticulous planning. It is worthwhile to invest a part of your time for planning first rather than directly starting to execute the tasks. When you prepare such a list, you are clearly focused and aligned towards your goals. In fact, one of the benefits of goal-setting is effective time management.

While preparing the list, allow some time for the fact that things don't always work out as scheduled and there are bound to be some deviations. Of course, the deviations will be minimized when you try to follow the list as closely as possible.

Revise your "to-do" list regularly by changing the priorities and eliminating the redundant activities. At the end of the day take a feedback on the execution of all the planned activities. If any major or important activity is left out, you can carry it forward to the next day for execution. And whenever you find any extra time available, you can execute some other action, depending on the priority.

Set Time for Each Task

Set a fixed time-frame for completion of each task so that you spend your time wisely. For instance, spend one hour for walking every day, or jogging, or at the gym, but don't exceed this time as it will affect other scheduled tasks. Fix some time for checking mails or internet every day, or other important tasks. This will help you to focus on your important activities and also to spend your time judiciously.

Follow Your Biological Clock

Understand your biological clock. People are more productive at different times of the day. They must be able to spot their moods and productive time periods and must work on tasks accordingly. When they are in their more productive period, they get better ideas or are able to find solutions to difficult problems. They must spend this productive time especially for important activities. During other time periods they can plan to do routine things which do not require much of their mental energies or attention. This is possible only when people understand their biological clock well.

Learn to Delegate

Delegation is an excellent tool where leaders assign routine tasks to their subordinates. It helps their subordinates to grow as leaders by learning to do things by themselves and learning lessons from their mistakes. At the same time leaders find more time to concentrate on more important activities. This also helps them to grow as stronger and better leaders.

Use Your Travelling Time

You should try to use your travelling time productively. You can read a book or a magazine while travelling or while waiting to meet anyone. You can also check your emails or read articles on the internet on your areas of interest. You can also use this time to make phone calls to clients or catch up with your old friends or relatives.

Avoid Information Overload

These days a huge amount of information is available on the internet. Often, people find it tough to differentiate between what is necessary and what is unnecessary. John C. Maxwell says in his book *Success—What Every Leader Needs to Know*, "More new information has been produced in the last thirty years than in the previous five thousand. A single weekday edition of *The New York Times* contains more information than most people in seventeenth-century England were likely to encounter in their lifetimes."

Studies reveal that now knowledge gets doubled annually, unlike in the 19th century where it took almost 100 years. Too much of information clutters the minds and results in wastage of precious time. It has become a problem of plenty for all of us. For freeing the mind from clutter, Jim Collins says in his book, *Good to Great*, "Most of us lead busy, but undisciplined lives. We have ever-expanding 'to do' lists, trying to build momentum by doing, doing, doing—and doing more. And it rarely works. Those who build the good-to-great companies, however, made as much use of "stop doing" lists as the "to do" lists. They displayed a remarkable amount of discipline to unplug all sorts of extraneous junk."

Hence, avoid information overload. This will not only save your time but also fine-tune your mind and polish your personality.

Think of Smart Work

Although hard work is essential for achieving the desired outcomes, you must also emphasize on smart work to achieve the outcomes within a limited time-frame. Whenever you want to perform any task, question yourself as to what can be the multiple outcomes out of your efforts and investments. This will help you to set the correct priorities and provide solutions to the problems. Hence, always question yourself before you start any activity. This will save not only your energy but also your time and money.

Discuss Ideas, not Individuals

It is rightly said that below-average persons discuss individuals, average persons discuss issues and above-average persons discuss ideas. When you discuss too much about individuals, you get into unnecessary controversies and into negative zone. In contrast, when you discuss ideas you get appreciation and command the respect of others as you present yourself as constructive and creative. And leaders emphasize more on ideas than on individuals when they troubleshoot or resolve various organizational issues.

Educators and Time Management

Educators must make proper use of their time in the classrooms. They must plan their teaching sessions carefully. They must remember that if they teach 20 students for an hour, the total time spent is 21 hours, which is a lot of time. Hence, they must do a lot of research, sequence and structure the content of their classroom sessions effectively to ensure that the students achieve the learning goals. This will save the time of both the students and the educators.

Emphasize Similarities, Not Differences

Employees in the workplace and people in their personal lives waste their precious time by focusing on differences rather than on similarities which connect them together. When people emphasize on similarities rather than differences, they build bridges and promote goodwill. In contrast, when people emphasize more on differences of opinions or ideas or views, they build barriers which result in breakup of relationships.

In fact, difference of opinion is an indication of independence and freedom among people. Voltaire said, "I may not agree with what you have to say, but I'll defend to my death your right to say it." Hence, we must always respect differences of opinions as people are different and have different emotions, egos, feelings, ideas, and insights. Even twins are not alike in their views and ideas. We must always appreciate the different opinions of others. Try to look at similarities rather than differences to maintain healthy relations.

To conclude, time is an irreplaceable resource. It is more than money. If you waste one second of your time you wasted that part of your precious life as God gave us a limited lifespan.

12

Delegate Effectively

"The best executive is the one who has sense enough to pick good men to do what he wants done, and self-restraint enough to keep from meddling with them while they do it."

Theodore Roosevelt

Some supervisors try to do everything by themselves. This may be due to lack of trust in their subordinates' capabilities or apprehension that their subordinates may grow in their positions and eventually overtake them. Sometimes the supervisors don't know how to delegate the tasks effectively. This results in increase of their workload and stress as they are often unable to meet their deadlines. This may also result in a communication gap between the supervisors and subordinates. Therefore, the solution for the supervisors lies in delegating the tasks effectively and efficiently to their subordinates.

What is Delegation?

Delegation is assigning tasks to qualified people without specifying too many details about execution so that the people will be able to apply their own methods, means, and knowledge to execute them. In this process, the superiors do not interfere in the execution of the tasks, except for supervising, guiding, and facilitating them.

Delegation is a smart work where the superiors hand over their routine, time consuming, and less challenging tasks to their subordinates. It helps both the leaders as well as the subordinates. The leaders find time to concentrate on key and challenging tasks by passing on less significant tasks to their subordinates. The subordinates get an opportunity to prove themselves and grow as leaders. Hence, it is a win-win for both leaders and followers. The former grow rapidly to the next higher position as more time is created for them to do critical jobs while the latter can also grow to the next higher level by acquiring competencies and capabilities during execution of the delegated tasks.

Delegation does not mean dumping work on others. It should not be confused with task allocation or task assignment. Delegation involves the delegators giving authority and responsibility to do certain tasks to others, while task allocation involves assigning roles and responsibilities to others without giving the authority.

Importance of Delegation

"The first rule of management is delegation. Don't try and do everything yourself because you can't." — Anthea Turner
Delegation is an effective leadership tool that leaders must understand and make use of. It helps in many ways such as creating more time for leaders, making others more accountable, empowering them, allowing them to experiment and learn lessons, and grooming them to become competent superiors and leaders. We will discuss this in detail.

Delegation helps you in managing your time effectively. The routine activities can be delegated to those subordinates who can do them without compromising on quality. The time so saved can be utilized for other productive activities.

You can also delegate the tasks which relate to your areas of weaknesses. We all have our strengths and weaknesses and delegating tasks for which we do not have strengths helps to avoid mistakes and also to empower subordinates. For instance, if you are not a good speaker and there is a need to deliver a speech, you can delegate the task to one of your subordinates who is good at public speaking. This will help both the delegator and the subordinate, as the delegator avoids mistakes and the subordinate feel empowered and recognized. However, do not delegate tasks to your subordinates where both of you have similar weaknesses, as it will lead to failure.

Delegation helps in grooming your subordinates for leadership roles. It enhances their confidence as they see that they are competent to execute things independently. Neale Donald Walsch said, "A true Master is not the one with the most students, but one who creates the most Masters. A true leader is not the one with the most followers, but one who creates the most leaders." The subordinates begin respecting you as a leader when you trust them and delegate important tasks to them.

Delegation helps in the effective utilization of human resources. It helps in capitalizing the strengths of the people around you. People will be happy when they are recognized for their talents and skills. As a leader, you will also be happy as, when you empower them, you save your time and groom your successors as well. Delegation also helps in proper distribution of work among the group members.

Delegation enhances trust among the group members. It bridges the gap between the superiors and subordinates, promotes fraternity, and leads to increased productivity.

Delegation reduces your stress since you reduce your workload by sharing it. It elevates the self-image and self-esteem of your subordinates. Your subordinates acquire professional competencies and capabilities to excel as leaders in the future.

According to the American psychologist Abraham Maslow, there is a hierarchy of needs in every individual. Every human being wants to satisfy them in order of priority. These needs are—physiological needs, safety needs, social needs, self-esteem needs and, on the top of the pyramid, self-actualization needs. Delegation helps to fulfil the social and self-esteem needs, paving the way for self-actualization.

Delegation helps people to learn their lessons by actually doing things. You need to spend a lot of ammunition to excel as an expert shooter. Similarly, you can acquire competencies only when you perform actual tasks. No amount of theory can substitute for actual experience. Theory may help you to some extent only, as you can learn from the experience of others.

Apart from bringing several benefits to both the delegator and the subordinate, delegation also brings several benefits to the organization, such as operational efficiency, professionalism, fraternity, and minimizing the operating costs.

Finally, delegation helps to enhance employee engagement as they become more committed to their work and acquire the requisite competencies and capabilities.

Challenges to Delegation

"No person will make a great business who wants to do it all himself or get all the credit." —Andrew Carnegie

Lester Urwick says in *Elements of Administration*, "Without delegation no organization can function effectively. Yet, lack of courage to delegate properly, and the knowledge of how to do it, is one of the most general causes of failure in organizations."

Often, it takes a lot of time to explain the tasks to the subordinates. Even then, lack of understanding on their part may result in improper execution. Sometimes leaders think it is more convenient to do the tasks by themselves rather than go through the trouble of delegation. Some leaders may avoid delegation for fear of delay or mistakes by their subordinates for, eventually, they are responsible for the results.

Sometimes subordinates do not welcome the extra work for fear that it may become a regular practice for superiors to increase their burden. Therefore, they say "No" quickly to delegation. It is also possible that subordinates don't have the requisite mindset, skills, or tools to execute the tasks. At times *fear of failure* and *fear of criticism* force the subordinates to avoid trying new things, resulting in ineffective delegation.

Sometimes leaders don't delegate for fear of losing their importance. This shows their lack of self-confidence. In fact, leadership involves encouraging others and handholding the competent to take them to the next higher level. When we look at Level 5 leadership, as explained by Jim Collins, the Level 5 leaders don't mind giving the credit for the job done and they do this with professionalism and humility.

Delegation Tips

- Be clear about what you are delegating. Tell your people clearly the motive and objectives behind the delegation to enable them to know clearly what your expectations are. Hence, communication is very important in delegation. After clarifying your expectations from the assigned tasks, ask a few questions to check whether your people have understood your instructions and expectations clearly. If you find a gap in their understanding, repeat your instructions clearly and then take a feedback once again. Ambiguity in communication can prove to be counterproductive, resulting in delays in execution and wasting of precious time. In addition, make sure that you delegate an entire task, not in pieces, as it helps others to look at it holistically for effective execution.
- After delegation, if you find that the person is unable to execute the task properly, find out the reason and

Delegate Effectively

advise the person how to solve the problems. But, if possible, don't hand over the task to someone else as it will demoralize the first person.

- Select carefully what you would like to delegate. Prepare a list of what you should do yourself and what requires less focus on your part and hence can be delegated.
- Make sure that the right kind of people are in your team. Check for their attitude, aptitude, and strengths and allot the roles and responsibilities to them accordingly.
- Bring awareness among your group members so that they can identify clearly what is urgent and important.
- George S. Patton said, "Never tell people how to do things. Tell them what to do and they will surprise you with their ingenuity." Tell your people what to do but don't tell them how to do it. Every person has his own way of doing things. Sometimes they may do them even better than you! This also helps you to learn newer methods of doing things. Besides, some people do not appreciate being spoon-fed. They don't like the leaders micromanaging them. They want to have freedom to execute the tasks according to their preferences.
- If required, boost the morale of your group members from time to time.
- If people fail, don't criticize. Allow them to experiment and learn lessons from their failures.
- After successful execution of a task, reward the person publicly for the achievement. This serves as a good example for others to follow.
- Have patience. Your people may not be an expert like you and they may take a little longer time than what you would take. But, after some time, you may be surprised to see how well they execute the tasks through their creativity and imagination.

- Don't accept inferior work or work which was done incorrectly or wrongly. If you find that a task was not performed properly, make sure that you communicate it clearly. Then demonstrate how to do it correctly and then get it done again. Delegation does not mean accepting incorrect or inferior output.

If these tips are followed, the organization can enhance its productivity within the available resources. Remember, it is the bad tradesman who blames his tools. The good tradesman delivers the best within the available resources.

Tale of My Two Sons

My two sons—Ganesh Sai and Ramakrishna Sayee—when they were in school, were very dependent on their mother. As they grew older, I thought it was time to make them independent and confident. I started to delegate small tasks and explained how to perform them. Initially, they were hesitant to accept the new responsibilities. So I encouraged and motivated them. For instance, when they wanted to buy some books, I helped them to find the way to the bookshop by searching Google maps and also told them how to negotiate for a better price. After they came back, I asked them about their experience and gave suggestions so that they could handle things better the next time.

There are several lessons that can be learned better through experience. And my two sons learnt by trial and error and thus developed leadership skills and abilities. They now advise and support their friends, working as leaders in the school and in their social circle. Although initially they had resisted doing things by themselves, their respect for me increased when they realized what I was teaching them. They became more confident and excelled as leaders within their network.

It is rightly said, "Even 'Super-You' needs help and support. There is no shame in asking for assistance. Push aside the pride and show respect for the talent others can bring to the table. And, remember that there is no such thing as a single-handed success: When you include and acknowledge all those in your corner, you propel yourself, your teammates, and your supporters to greater heights." Hence, the next time you find that you have a lot of pressure because of work or feel that you are stressed out, adopt this wonderful leadership tool of delegation which brings benefits to you and to the people around you.

13

Empower People

"Excellence breeds character, and character breeds excellence. Demand excellence from your people, and they will develop into people who also demand excellence of themselves and the people they lead."

John C. Maxwell

One of the methods used by leaders for effective leadership is to empower people around them to enable their development as leaders. John Maxwell, in his book *Developing the Leaders around You*, emphasizes the importance of empowerment. In fact, great leaders handhold their people and develop them to avoid any leadership vacuum and to take their organizations to next higher level. They emphasize more on the longevity of the institutions rather than of the individuals. In this chapter we will discuss the importance of empowerment.

What is Empowerment?

"Don't use your people to build a great work; use your work to built great people." — Jack Hyles

Empowerment is to give responsible freedom to people to explore and execute tasks, after making the right decisions.

Empowerment is a partnership where both leaders and team members work in a focused manner for achieving the organizational objectives. According to Karakoc, "Empowerment is to give more authority to employees in organization in management of work."

Empowerment must be treated as a leadership tool where leaders develop their people by giving them powers to take decisions. It helps people to build confidence since they make decisions and execute things by themselves. And if something goes wrong, the leaders are there to help and support them.

Empowerment should not be confused with bosses giving up their powers and employees giving away their freedom. Empowerment is delegation of power to the juniors. It reduces the concentration of power in the hands of a few seniors. It enhances employees' engagement and they feel truly valued by the organization.

However, empowerment has both advantages as well as disadvantages.

Importance of Empowerment

Empowerment is necessary in any organization as it encourages employees to take initiative, take decisions and execute plans. Often, the operational people know the ground realities much better than the top management. Hence, empowering people at each level of hierarchy helps them to take decisions and take actions according to the need of the situation.

Empowerment enhances the knowledge, skills, and abilities of employees as they develop competencies and capabilities quickly. Apart from raising the self-esteem of the employees, it also trains them for higher positions. It ensures smooth succession. It enhances loyalty towards the organization. Above all, empowerment enables the employees to make a significant contribution to the organization.

Delegation vs. Empowerment

"Power can be taken, but not given. The process of the taking is empowerment in itself." —Gloria Steinem

Delegation is how you allot your tasks and activities to your subordinates so that you can save your time and concentrate on other important tasks that need your attention. Usually, routine or less important tasks are delegated. Delegation helps your team members to acquire competencies and capabilities. Delegation can also involve handing over the tasks for which you do not have strengths to perform, provided your subordinates have the requisite strengths.

On the other hand, empowerment is to give powers to your team members to enable them to take decisions and execute the plans. However, you still need to supervise the work to avoid any mistakes which may be committed by your team members. Empowerment helps your team members to excel as leaders in the long run.

Although both delegation and empowerment appear to be similar, they are actually quite different. The common aspect connected with them is participation. Both allow the people to participate in decision making so that they feel valued and respected and a part of the management.

So delegation is to pass on the tasks to competent subordinates. Empowerment is to give powers to others to take decisions and execute the plans.

In delegation, the team members must inform about the results of the tasks performed to the delegators. However, in empowerment the team members can take their own decisions and there is no need to provide feedback on the tasks to the person who empowered them.

Empowerment helps people more than delegation. Delegation is temporary. In empowerment, people will have more freedom and powers to do things by themselves compared to delegation, where people will often receive instructions about the tasks to be performed.

Every organization has goals to achieve and empowerment helps people to determine their own means, strategies, tools and techniques to achieve their goals. Empowerment gives freedom to explore, experiment, and execute the tasks. Of course, all this has to be done according to the organization's ethics and moral code. In contrast, delegation does not give such freedom and asks the employees to execute the tasks according to the directions or instructions of the delegator.

Delegation lays emphasis on policies, procedures, control, and direction while empowerment lays emphasis on outcomes and achievements. Delegation builds managerial skills among the people while empowerment builds leadership skills. Delegation is means oriented while empowerment is goal oriented. Above all, delegation emphasizes on giving authority to the employee while empowerment emphasizes on giving responsibility.

Peter Drucker said, "No executive has ever suffered because his subordinates were strong and effective." Leaders must realize that they lose nothing by empowering others. Actually, they gain respect from them.

Empowerment is not a new concept. During the American Civil War, Abraham Lincoln empowered his military commander, Ulysses S. Grant and sent him a message, "I neither ask nor desire to know anything of your plans. Take the responsibility and act and call me if you need assistance."

To sum up, in the words of U.S. President Woodrow Wilson, "You are not here merely to make a living. You are here in order to enable the world to live more amply, with greater vision, with a finer spirit of hope and achievement. You are here to enrich the world, and to impoverish yourself if you forget the errand."

14

Be Open to Feedback

"Be open to feedback. A CEO should be evaluated on a regular basis. It's the best thing that can happen to a CEO because if you're failing, then you need to know about it. If you are getting high ratings, and someone says you're not doing a good job, then they're off base and you have the data to prove it."

Raymond D. Fowler, PhD

Good leaders are open to feedback. Marshall Goldsmith in his book, *What Got You Here Won't Get You There—How Successful People Become Even More Successful* emphasized the importance of feedback. Ken Blanchard said, "Feedback is the breakfast of champions."

Leaders take feedback from all sources to enhance their performance and to have a wider acceptance from others. Feedback is also used by leaders to develop themselves and for increasing their effectiveness.

All human beings have blind spots. Unless they accept feedback, they cannot know about them and bring about behavioural changes to improve themselves. Organizations use this leadership development tool for enhancing the productivity and performance of their employees. However, research reveals that a majority of the people do not take feedback in a constructive manner, especially if it is viewed as a criticism by them. When the feedback is positive, they feel happy, but the moment it becomes negative, they become defensive and point fingers at the person giving the feedback. Abraham Lincoln believed that his rivals provided the best feedback which improved his leadership capabilities.

Feedback is neither criticism nor praise, though some people may believe otherwise. Feedback is a result of how a person, or his behaviour or actions, are perceived by others which, at times, he may not know himself. Thus, feedback serves as a tool for the development of individuals and should not be misunderstood as either criticism or praise.

Feedback has two aspects—giving feedback and receiving feedback. Some people may think that receiving feedback is more difficult than giving feedback. The fact is that both giving and receiving feedback effectively is difficult. Here are some tips for giving feedback.

Tips to give Feedback

Leaders must make sure that they provide feedback to others in an objective manner and specify clearly the areas where behavioural changes are needed.

While giving feedback, focus on the behaviour, not on the individual. If you focus on the individual, there will be a resistance to receive the feedback. Hence, depersonalize your criticism. Make it objective and specific. Don't hurt people. Make the feedback as polite as possible so that the receiver takes it positively.

Avoid the usage of the words *"always"* and *"never"* as they can cause problems. Replace them with *"often"* and *"sometimes"* as these words can help to increase the acceptance of the feedback.

Give feedback as soon as you notice the issue as it makes things clearer for both the giver and the receiver of the feedback. Delay in giving feedback can make it difficult for the receiver to understand the context and complicate the situation for both the giver and the receiver.

In the end, ask the receiver to summarize the feedback to confirm that he has understood it.

Tips to Receive Feedback

When you are receiving feedback, don't get defensive. Listen carefully, with a correct body language and with an open mind. At the end, smile and thank the person for his time and effort.

Don't react to the feedback negatively. Listen carefully, without getting offended. There is an inner noise or dialogue that takes place among all human beings. Suspend that dialogue during this time so that you become a good listener. Don't try to argue with the giver of the feedback.

Swallow your pride when you hear something which is not positive. Excessive pride ruins the prospects of growth. Hence, keep your pride aside and accept the feedback.

Seek suggestions for improvement from the giver of the feedback. This will show your positive attitude in receiving feedback.

Evaluate the feedback carefully and see if you have received a similar feedback earlier. If it is so, then it is time to make the desired changes immediately.

When someone gives you feedback, it shows that they care about you. You must be happy that he thinks, cares and is concerned about you. If you understand this, you will take the feedback positively.

Always thank the person for providing you feedback. Accept the feedback if it is objective and specific. If you find that if a correction is needed in your behaviour, do it immediately. In this way you will be able to enhance your abilities.

Informal Feedback

"If you don't get feedback from your performers and your audience, you're going to be working in a vacuum." — Peter Maxwell Davies

Often, informal feedback is more beneficial than formal feedback. This is so because there are many things that cannot be expressed during formal feedback. This is the reason why many leaders spend a lot of time talking to their people informally. Many CEOs travel extensively to interact directly with their managers and to receive their feedback. Some leaders believe more in informal rather than formal feedback.

As a teacher, I depend on informal feedback from my students to improve my teaching. I ask my students, through open-ended questions, about the changes that need to be made in my lessons or teaching style. I start by asking them about what they liked the most in my teaching and then gradually ask for ideas on changes that may be needed. I ask these questions outside the class, as some students may not open up during the class. Sometimes students ask me to cover the syllabus rather than spend time on the industry experiences. Some students ask me to give more information on career options to help them to choose the right careers. They also ask me to include stories and case studies that can help them to understand the challenges faced by organizations. In this manner, students express their needs and expectations informally.

Thus, we have seen that informal feedback is important for both leaders and their team members.

Feedback to Students

Feedback is important everywhere. Students get feedback from teachers and teachers get feedback from students. The intention of any feedback is to make people, policies, practices, systems, or structures better.

While giving feedback to your students, you have to be a little more careful. The students expect to receive positive feedback from their teachers and they like to be praised in the front of other students. As far as possible, don't hurt their egos in the classroom. If you find that there is a need for major changes in their behaviour, the best thing to do is to call them separately and provide them feedback to improve.

While giving feedback, use the "sandwich feedback" style. Sandwich feedback is to put a negative thing in between two positive things. It all starts with a compliment, followed by the behaviour that needs correction and concludes with a compliment. As a feedback giver, you will gain the respect of the receiver for giving this kind of a feedback and the receiver will accept the feedback constructively.

While giving feedback, make sure that you criticize the behaviour rather than the person. Such approach makes the feedback more meaningful and effective. For instance, let me share my experience when I presided as a judge for a paper presentation competition at a college.

Sarah's Body Language

Sarah was a bright student who presented a paper during the competition. I was evaluating each student based on six parameters—depth of knowledge, communication skills, body language, time management, confidence, and the ability to handle the question-and-answer session. Most of the students did not score well on two or three parameters. At the end of the competition, Sarah met me and enquired about her presentation. Instead of giving her the feedback in front of others, I asked her to meet me separately.

When Sarah met me, I gave her a sandwich feedback.

Sarah, the way you presented the topic was interesting. You covered the topic in depth. This shows that you worked hard and researched the topic well. You made the presentation unique with interesting examples and held the attention of the audience throughout the presentation. Your communication skills are also good and you made the presentation with confidence.

However, while delivering the presentation your body language was negative and the way you stood was awkward. If you have the time, you can make a video recording of a trial presentation and observe and improve the body postures.

And let me add, you managed your time well and you completed your presentation on time. This shows that you practiced your presentation many times. You also handled the question-and-answer session with tact and diplomacy. Overall, your presentation was good.

After listening to my sandwich feedback, Sarah got a clear message and said, "Sir, thanks for your feedback. Now I realize that I must improve my body language and posture. As you suggested, I will rehearse my presentation and record it. I will improve my awkward body language and posture. Thank you for giving me the right feedback."

Giving feedback is a very challenging task. Don't misuse the opportunity to give feedback for your personal ends or to settle scores with your rivals. View feedback as a tool for the development and benefit of others. Feedback should be objective, specific, impartial, and constructive.

15

Blend both Hard and Soft Skills

"The softest things in the world overcome the hardest things in the world."
Lao-Tzu

Leaders must learn to blend both soft and hard skills to enhance their leadership effectiveness. Focusing either on soft skills or hard skills only does not produce a balanced leader. The right blend of both soft and hard skills is essential to achieve leadership excellence. We will explore this in this chapter.

Soft and Hard Skills

According to the psychologist Daniel Goleman, soft skills are a combination of competencies that contribute to a person's ability to manage himself and relate to other people. These are the skills, abilities, and traits about the personality, attitude, and behaviour of a person. Soft skills are twice as important as IQ or technical skills for the success of a person.

There is often a misunderstanding that soft skills reflect the "softness" of the person. People often equate soft skills with communication skills and emotional intelligence. The truth is that soft skills are much more than that. Soft skills include team building skills, negotiation skills, leadership skills, time management skills, critical thinking skills, ability to manage conflict, motivation, social graces, and etiquette. In contrast, hard skills are the core skills like domain knowledge and technical competency needed to execute tasks effectively.

There is a big difference between soft and hard skills. Soft skills emphasize on how one speaks while hard skills emphasize on what one speaks. For instance, saying *"Thanks for not using the telephone"* uses soft skills while saying, *"Telephone should not be used"* uses hard skills. Soft skills are used to convey the message in a polite and pleasing manner while hard skills are used just to communicate the message.

There are people who are removed from their jobs due to their negative attitude even though they are competent technically. People are always hired and promoted for their positive attitude. During the interview for a job, the interviewer often emphasizes more on attitude than skills, though skills are equally important. There is an HR adage, *"Hire for attitude and train for skill"*. Attitude is an important ingredient of soft skills and it can be cultivated through right awareness, training, and practice.

It is rightly said that people rise in their positions in an organization due to hard skills and fall due to dearth of soft skills. Some people think that their technical competence alone is sufficient to excel professionally. This is incorrect. Here is the story of Susan, who had hard skills but lacked soft skills, as an illustration.

Susan was a hard working woman. She was punctual and a dedicated employee of an IT company. She was a team leader and 15 people reported to her. She had good technical knowledge and even her seniors would consult her whenever there was a technical problem. But she found it difficult to manage people. She believed in perfection and expected her team members to do the same. She was very harsh with people who were habitually late to office. Most of her subordinates were unhappy with her style of functioning and her rigid behaviour. Two team members were so vexed with her that they quit the company. The others did not follow her instructions and there was a drop in the performance of the team.

The matter came to the notice of the HR department. After a detailed review, Susan was transferred to another department, without any supervisory responsibilities.

From this example, it is clear that being a technical expert alone is not sufficient to be a good leader. Leaders must learn to get along with others, empathize with them, and demonstrate flexibility. It is also clear that being good only at hard skills is not sufficient and it is essential to have soft skills to ensure professional growth and success.

Ram Charan outlines the importance of both business acumen and people acumen for leaders in his book, *Leaders At All Levels*. He says, "Anyone can improve his or her ability to select and develop people's talents, but the other aspects of people acumen are hard to teach. Leaders with people acumen have good instincts to anticipate problems among individuals who must work together, and to get them resolved. When leaders are unable to make good decisions, or any decisions at all, it may be that their business acumen is not expanding. They cannot be considered to have CEO potential." Here business acumen is the same as hard skills and people acumen the same as soft skills. We can also say that hard skills include IQ (Intelligent Quotient) and soft skills include EQ (Emotional Quotient). A blend of both is needed for achieving success.

It is essential for leaders to acquire and constantly improve their skills, abilities, competencies, and capabilities to lead their teams to success. Carole Nicola Ides said, "In today's competitive environment, it is not enough to be the best in your field, intellectually. Competency is only half of what you need to climb the ladder of success. The other half is the softer side of you—it's that part of you that will be liked, admired, trusted, and remembered."

16

Humility Goes Before Honour

"I have three precious things which I hold fast and prize. The first is gentleness; the second frugality; the third is humility, which keeps me from putting myself before others. Be gentle and you can be bold; be frugal and you can be liberal; avoid putting yourself before others and you can become a leader among men."

Lao-Tzu

When you look at great leaders like Mahatma Gandhi, Dalai Lama, and Mother Teresa, there is one common trait among them—humility. Inspite of their status, their humility remained intact. In this chapter we will see how humility paves the way to great leadership.

Humility and Leadership

Humility is not a sign of weakness. Charles H. Spurgeon said, "Humility is to make a right estimate of oneself." Humility is neither inferiority nor superiority. It is neither weakness nor submissiveness. It is finding self-worth within you, with limited ego, and unlimited generosity, to handhold and help others. It is making you accessible to others, without false ego or prestige. It is being open to receiving feedback from all sources, young and old, senior and junior, without ego, for successful decision making.

Inferior quality leaders are usually not humble as they try to mask their insecurities with overt self promotion, not accepting responsibility, and blaming others for their mistakes. They try to take credit when things go right and pass the blame to others when things go wrong.

Good leaders are aware that it is essential to have humility. But excessive humility is perceived by others as a weakness and lack of humility can be perceived as pride. Sun Tzu defined leadership as a matter of intelligence, trustworthiness, humaneness, courage, and discipline. However, reliance on intelligence alone results in rebelliousness; exercise of humaneness alone results in weakness; fixation on trust results in folly; dependence on the strength or courage results in violence; excessive discipline and sternness in command results in rebellion. When one has all the five virtues together, in the correct balance, each appropriate to its function, then only can one be a good leader.

Humility—From Good to Great

"We come nearest to the great when we are great in humility." —Rabindranath Tagore

To progress from a good to a great leader, Jim Collins says that two key attributes are required—personal humility and professional will. These are the keys to Level 5 leadership. Level 5 leaders shun public attention and are not boastful. They handhold and help others. They derive pleasure when others make progress. They consider others' progress as their own and don't hanker after rewards.

Thus, it is clear that humility is the key to effectiveness and greatness as a leader. According to Jim Collins, "Abraham Lincoln was the last Level 5 President the US has had. He was reserved, awkward, gangly, and had personal humility. But he had a goal of preserving the Union even if 600,000 people, including himself, had to die to accomplish that."

Get On, Get Honest, and Get Honour

Humility is one of the key ingredients of effective leadership. All great leaders exhibit this trait. The higher they rise, the higher is their humility index!

There are three stages of any person—*Get On, Get Honest,* and *Get Honour.* Initially a person struggles for getting on with his life. This stage is known as "*Get On*". Once the person achieves some success, he adopts the right tools and techniques, emphasizes on ethics and etiquette to grow in his life. This stage is known as "*Get Honest*". After reaching this position, the person strives for being admired by others and emphasizes on principles and ethics. This stage is known as "*Get Honour*". At this stage the person keeps others' interests above his own interests. Hence, *Get On, Get Honest,* and *Get Honour* are the three stages in the life of any successful person.

Academic Arrogance

Some academicians have high egos. They have a large number of papers published in leading publications. This leads to academic arrogance. Such people must realize that an attitude of arrogance prevents further academic growth. Marshall Goldsmith outlines this in a different context in his book *What got you here won't get you there.* He says, "Those who are successful should not take further success for granted. What worked in the past may not work in the future. Be open to feedback and keep changing your tools and techniques to reach further higher positions with humility."

Vicente Fox, former president of Mexico, says on humility, "The higher leaders rise, the further they move from where they began. The danger is that success will undermine their humility, leaving them out of touch and disconnected. . . . There are so many temptations that would undermine your humility. You have to develop that part, work on it all your life. It's easy to fall on the other side, especially when you are in power and have a position."

All academicians must recognize the fact that the higher they rise, the higher must be their humility index. They cannot consider themselves to be super beings. They must learn the difference between ego and arrogance. Similarly, when some people have more knowledge, they want the entire world to salute them. This is an incorrect attitude. They must know that the knowledge acquired has to be shared and used for the benefit of all and not be a reason for boasting and pride.

Humility vs. Arrogance

"Pride is concerned with who is right. Humility is concerned with what is right." — Ezra Taft Benson

Humble people know that it is the humility that gets honour, not the other way round. What they don't know, they must ask others and learn. They know that arrogance is the biggest enemy of humility. They acknowledge their weaknesses and work to overcome them, instead of hiding behind justifications and defending them. Above all, they admit their mistakes, listen more, talk less, appreciate others, and contribute their best. John J. McCloy said, "Humility leads to strength and not to weakness. It is the highest form of self-respect to admit mistakes and to make amends for them." Leaders must realize that humility is the journey towards honour. All great leaders reached their levels of greatness only through their humility.

To conclude, leaders must know that their humility index must increase as their age, experience, and success increase. Given the choice between honour and humility, humility takes precedence. It is humility which is supreme. When leaders make humility as the cornerstone of their lives, they receive honour and are acknowledged as great leaders.

17

A Good Leader is a Great Servant

"The first responsibility of a leader is to define reality. The last is to say thank you. In between, the leader is a servant."

Max DePree

There are several leaders who make a difference to the lives of others through their extraordinary contributions towards the society. One such person was Florence Nightingale, the Lady with the Lamp. She served with compassion, commitment, and an attitude of service. She is a good example of the statement that a good leader is a great servant.

Florence Nightingale—Profile

Florence Nightingale became a nurse despite stiff opposition from her parents. In those days, nurses were not treated with respect. It was believed that drunkards and people with little merit joined the profession as a last resort, when they had no other means to earn their livelihood. If the nursing profession is respected today, it is due to her dedicated services.

She was a very cool and calm leader, with a pleasant disposition, which helped patients to forget their sufferings and pain. She made a huge difference to the lives of the wounded and sick soldiers. More than a century ago, she proved that women were not the "weaker sex" and that they were capable of great acts. As a woman leader, she made a position for herself as a symbol of servant leadership, a phrase coined by Robert Greenleaf subsequently.

Florence Nightingale

A True Servant Leader

"I think one's feelings waste themselves in words; they ought all to be distilled into actions which bring results." — Florence Nightingale

Florence Nightingale is a good example of a servant leader. She left her comfortable life at home to serve the soldiers wounded in the Crimean war. Norman Vincent Peale has said, "The man who lives for himself is a failure; the man who lives for others has achieved true success." Florence achieved success through her compassion and commitment. She set an excellent example for others to follow.

She not only served the patients well, but also led the nurses from the front. She was assertive while handling the nurses who were addicted to alcohol and other vices. She helped to reduce the mortality rate of soldiers substantially by her care of the wounded. Now-a-days we talk of leadership training programmes. However, she conducted nurses' training programmes way back in 1860.

Nursing Legend

The nursing profession is a kind of servant leadership, where the nurses are dedicated to the cause of serving the patients. It requires serving the patients through a selfless attitude. Only servant leaders can be successful in the nursing profession. These leaders should have passion, patience, kindness, empathy, selflessness, and commitment. Florence Nightingale became a legend and elevated the prestige of the nursing profession through her practical involvement and commitment. Here is what *The Times* said in her praise:

She is a "ministering angel" without any exaggeration in these hospitals, and as her slender form glides quietly along each corridor, every poor fellow's face softens with gratitude at the sight of her. When all the medical officers have retired for the night and silence and darkness have settled down upon those miles of prostrate sick, she may be observed alone, with a little lamp in her hand, making her solitary rounds.

A Level 5 Leader

According to Jim Collins, Florence Nightingale was a Level 5 leader who symbolized professional will and personal humility. She demonstrated this when she returned from the Crimean war, without any fanfare. Since she would not sit in it, her empty carriage was paraded in the city of Southampton to honour her contribution during the war. Queen Victoria appreciated her and said, "You have no self-importance or humbug. No wonder the soldiers love you so." This is a description of a Level 5 leader.

Leadership Lessons

Here are the lessons we can learn from Florence Nightingale:
- Follow your passions. Don't be influenced by others because only you know where your strengths and

interests are. Follow your heart. Florence Nightingale had a passion to serve others and mitigate human suffering. Although there was a stiff opposition from her parents, she followed her heart and succeeded in her mission.

- Stick to principles and values. Leadership involves values and morals. People die but the values they represent remain forever. Hence, emphasize on principles and values and don't get tempted by short-term benefits.
- Leadership is all about setting an example to influence others. If you want to influence others, you must first set an example for them to follow.
- You should understand that not taking a risk is also a risk. Leadership involves taking a lot of risk. During the Crimean war, Florence Nightingale took a great risk and entered the war zone. She bravely risked her life and served the wounded.
- Be compassionate. Compassion is the key to servant leadership.

Leadership is about standing up for your convictions even when the odds are stacked against you. Florence Nightingale stood for her values and convictions in the 19th century at a time there were no supporters to her cause. In the end, she proved that she was right and her critics were wrong. She remains a leadership icon and role model for nurses and other professionals.

Florence Nightingale falls in the category of great women leaders such as Eleanor Roosevelt, Frances Hesselbein, and Mother Teresa. She was a visionary and saw the future much ahead of others. She is relevant now and will remain so in the future. We will always need nurses to mitigate the sufferings of the sick. She will continue to inspire everyone, not only as a nursing leader, but also as a servant leader. Although she died a century ago, she is still remembered since her impact on mankind has been profound. She left the world a better place than the one she inherited. Henry Longfellow wrote a poem in 1857 about her:

Lo! In that hour of misery
A lady with a lamp I see
Pass through the glimmering gloom,
And flit from room to room.

18

Learn and Grow Continuously

"Leadership and learning are indispensable to each other."
                                                    John F. Kennedy

Stephen R. Covey in his famous book, *The Seven Habits of Highly Effective People* mentioned that continuous learning was one of the habits that enables people to be effective. He termed it as "Sharpen the Saw". When we read the biographies of great leaders, it is clear that they became successful because of their continuous learning.

Benjamin Franklin is a good example of how continuous learning can pave the way for excelling as a multi-faceted personality. He was an inventor, author, and statesman. He said, "If you empty your purse in your head, no one can take it away from you. An investment in knowledge always pays the best interest."

Abraham Lincoln is another example. He had very little formal education, but proved to be one of the best American presidents due to his continuous learning.

Some leaders learn from books, some leaders learn from their experiences and some from both. The important thing

to understand is that they could become successful leaders because of their continuous learning.

Learning doesn't mean reading books alone. It includes personal experiences, observation, teaching, training, and many others. Indra Nooyi, CEO of PepsiCo, remarked about learning, "The one thing I have learned as a CEO is that leadership at various levels is vastly different.... As you move up the organization, the requirements for leading that organization doesn't grow vertically; they grow exponentially.... If you want to improve the organization, you have to improve yourself and the organization gets pulled up with you.... Just because you are a CEO, don't think you have landed. You must continually increase your learning, the way you think, and the way you approach the organization."

Teach to Learn

"We now accept the fact that learning is a lifelong process of keeping abreast of change. And the most pressing task is to teach people how to learn." — Peter Drucker

It is often said that leaders are readers. It is also said that leaders are teachers and they learn many things while teaching others. Many successful leaders take time off from their busy schedules to teach executives and students. This not only helps them to share what they know, it also helps them to learn from their students. It is said, "To teach is to learn twice."

Leaders are thinkers, doers, analysts, decision-makers, troubleshooters, and crisis managers. They acquire all these qualities only through continuous learning. They keep updating their knowledge constantly. If leaders are not learners then it is impossible for them to lead.

Whether educated or uneducated, all leaders learn by trying, failing, falling, correcting and growing. And often they learn from the experiences of others. John Maxwell went a step ahead and said that the moment we stop learning, we stop leading.

Good Leaders vs. Great Leaders

Don't remain a specialist in a narrow domain as it becomes harder for you to grow in your career. Remember that leaders keep their minds open to new learning for achieving success. Leaders have to read and think deeply and widely to strike the right balance. By reading deeply you become an expert in your area and by reading widely you expand your mental horizons beyond your area of interest. We can say that good leaders read deeply and great leaders read both deeply and widely.

Peter Drucker laid out the basic principles of knowledge — work and the knowledge society. Of these, continuous learning is the most important. You can build on your strengths by incorporating continuous learning into everything you do. You can minimize your weaknesses by learning enough to do reasonably well at something that is not a part of your core competencies.

To modify a little what Mahatma Gandhi once said, when you are trying to learn, think that you will live long and you have a lot of time to get into the depth of the matter. When you are sharing your knowledge, think that you have no time at all, as if you will die the next moment and so you should pass on your accumulated knowledge as quickly as possible. This kind of thinking helps you to learn more and also to share more.

Sharpen Your Saw

If you want to stay ahead of others and to be successful, the only option available to you is to learn and grow continuously. Just as the body develops physically through regular exercise, the mind develops when you learn regularly.

19

Be a Transformational Leader

"A business short on capital can borrow money. But a business short of leadership has little chance of survival"

Peter Drucker

Every business has its unique challenges. However, it requires the right leaders and the right leadership styles to face the challenges successfully. In this chapter, we will discuss about transformational leadership, which helps to transform individuals and institutions to enable them to achieve greater success.

What is Transformational Leadership?

According to James MacGregor Burns, transformational leadership is a process in which "leaders and followers help each other to advance to a higher level of morale and motivation".

Transformational leadership is the process of developing the people, who, in turn, develop their organizations by accomplishing the determined goals and objectives. Although the achievement of goals is important, the methods adopted during the process are more important. In fact, this stress on means is what makes transformational leadership stand out from the other leadership styles.

Transformational leadership results in making ordinary people produce extraordinary performance. It enriches and reinforces values and ethics among the people. Transformational leaders are "myth makers" and "tale tellers", like charismatic leaders. However, they do not praise themselves, unlike charismatic leaders. They leave a rich legacy behind them, with suitable successors, unlike charismatic leaders who leave a leadership vacuum. They emphasize both means and ends, unlike transactional leaders who emphasize only ends.

"Transformational leadership recognizes and exploits an existing need or demand of a potential follower... (and) looks for potential motives in followers, seeks to satisfy higher needs, and engages the full person of the follower."
— James MacGregor Burns

Transformational leaders demonstrate trust and confidence in their team members and set high ethical and moral standards. They radiate energy and enthusiasm. They are comfortable working in teams. They believe in their people and their potential. They direct the energies of their people in the right directions to derive the best from them. Above all, these leaders emphasize more on means and ultimately accomplish their ends as well.

Leadership thinkers and researchers like Max Weber, MacGregor Burns, Bernard M. Bass, Warren Bennis, and Nanus have written extensively on this area of leadership.

Case Study on Transformational Leadership

Ron was a young leadership consultant and researcher who received a call from the Chairman of the Board of Directors of a private business college. Ron had done some consultancy work for him earlier, so the Chairman had a lot of trust and confidence in him. During the meeting, the Chairman narrated the problems faced by the college.

The Chairman had received many complaints about the Principal, Prof. James, and a senior faculty member, Prof. Susan. The Principal was perceived as weak and took a long time taking decisions or actions, even on important issues. Prof. Susan realized this and started influencing and controlling the decisions and actions of the Principal. Due to this, there were a lot of interpersonal problems between the teachers. The final result was that teaching and academic work suffered. Slowly, the research grants from the industry started to reduce and also the number of companies coming to the college for campus recruitment. The number of students applying for admission also started to fall. The Chairman feared that if no remedial action was taken immediately, the college may have to be closed.

Ron listened patiently to the problems and decided to take up the assignment. He promised to come up with a solution within a week.

After a week, Ron came back with his recommendations. He said that he had found the situation at the college to be terrible. The teaching work had come to a standstill. If no action was taken, the college would have to be closed right away. He proposed that both Prof. James and Prof. Susan be removed from their positions immediately. Since there was no time available to look for a new Principal, he offered his services on a three-year contract. But his remuneration would be high—almost four times of the amount being paid now.

The Board of Directors deliberated over the proposal for a long time. The scenario built by Ron was scary. They had allowed the situation to deteriorate by not taking action earlier. Now they had no option but to accept Ron's proposal. The fact that he was known to the Chairman was also taken into consideration.

So the services of Prof. James and Prof. Susan were terminated and Ron was appointed as the new Principal.

Solution

As expected, Ron was received with hostility as he was installed by the Board directly, without taking the opinion of the faculty members or any other stakeholders. Some senior professors felt that they could have been given the opportunity, especially in view of their long association with the college. However, Ron was unperturbed and moved ahead.

He met every faculty member and non-teaching staff individually and noted their concerns. He prepared a list of all the concerns and apprehensions and prioritized them according to their severity and importance. He made a time-bound action plan to resolve each one of them. When he announced this plan, everyone was amazed. They had not seen things moving at such a fast pace earlier.

The academic activities were already delayed by three weeks. There were no teachers for three subjects and the time table had to be prepared. Ron called a meeting of the entire faculty and asked for volunteers to teach the three subjects. Fortunately, Jack, who was a dedicated and committed professor, came forward and offered to shoulder the responsibility of handling one of the subjects. The other teachers were reluctant to take any extra load. Finally, by offering some monetary incentives, Ron could get a teacher to agree to teach the second subject. Since the situation was at a dead end, Ron decided to teach the third subject himself—he wanted to lead by example.

Ron realized that there was a lack of transparent and open communication between the management and the academic staff. Besides, there was no coordination between the marketing team that marketed the courses and the teachers. So he started a monthly meeting of the management team with the teachers and the marketing team. Everyone was allowed to raise the issues that concerned them for an immediate resolution.

During these meetings, Ron encouraged the team members to think creatively about the problems and their solutions. Often, the issues could be resolved by the team members themselves, without the intervention of the management.

Many good ideas and suggestions for improvement of the working of the college also emerged from these meetings. This started to develop a team spirit among all the members. They were motivated to look upon themselves as a single team where each member would help others to achieve their goals and objectives. This also contributed to making the working environment more positive.

While the above actions were underway, Ron gave a lot of attention to meeting the commitments he had given in the time bound action plan earlier. He referred to the list several times a day to ensure that even the smallest action was not left out. He knew that a leader has to deliver on his promises.

Ron infused confidence among the employees by replacing the prevailing pressure with pleasure, distrust with trust, and miscommunication with prompt and open communication.

During this period, Ron took initiatives in all areas. He identified the areas where there were gaps and addressed them. He did not shirk responsibility. He announced that the primary responsibility and accountability on any matter was his.

Ron also realized that the previous principal, Prof. James, had encouraged petty politics by favouring a few people and alienating the rest. He had been surrounded by sycophants. Ron changed all this. He ensured that everyone who had a stake in a decision was involved in the decision making process.

Ron made sure that the faculty members were always kept informed of all developments. He persuaded the administration department to take quick actions on all feedback. Gradually, a climate of trust and confidence was built up. Thus, Ron built bridges and removed the barriers.

During this time, two dissatisfied faculty members were found to be spreading rumours and negative stories. He quickly took a decision to fire them immediately, before the poison spread further. He made sure that everyone was informed of the real reason for the departure of these two persons to serve as a warning and also to ensure that no one could cause any misunderstandings.

Ron introduced several training and development programmes to enhance the skills of the faculty and the administrative staff. People felt valued and cared for with this gesture. This infused faith and confidence in them, opening the doors to better performance and growth.

Ron also arranged regular get-togethers of the students and teachers. The informal atmosphere allowed them to build better relationships. He explained to the teachers that the students were essential to their existence—if there were no students, there would be no teachers either!

Whenever any feedback emerged during these interactions, Ron ensured that action was taken. When a few students talked of problems with a particular teacher, he investigated the matter immediately. He found that the teacher was short tempered and would shout whenever he was asked questions in the class. Ron called him to his room and provided sandwich feedback to improve his behaviour. This had the desired result and the teacher's relationship with the students improved substantially. Ron's success in handling this case tactfully further enhanced the respect he commanded in the college.

Three years passed by quickly. When the Chairman reviewed the situation, he found that things had improved dramatically in the college. Industry grants had increased to record levels, a large number of students were applying to the college for admission, and the college had an enviable record of placing all its graduating students several months before their course ended. The number of research papers published by the faculty was at a record high. The atmosphere in the college was great. The faculty, administrative staff and the students had very good relationship with one another.

But there was a problem. The college was still losing money. The main reason was the high remuneration paid to Ron. So the Chairman was wondering what he should recommend to the Board—an extension to Ron or appoint another, less expensive person, maybe a senior faculty member of the college.

Bernard M. Bass's 4 I's

Ron effectively adopted the 4 I's of Bernard M. Bass, the leadership researcher—individualized consideration, intellectual stimulation, inspirational motivation and idealized influence.

He cared for his people. He empathized with their problems and solved them immediately. He recognized their motivational needs and acted accordingly. He stimulated his people intellectually by encouraging them to be creative and think out of the box in solving the challenges. He gave them freedom to do things in their own way and counselled them only when they were not able to resolve the issues themselves. He clearly articulated the vision of the institution and challenged the people by setting high standards. He demonstrated confidence and optimism. He displayed energy and enthusiasm throughout. He motivated his people continuously and constantly. Finally, he set an example by his own performance and became a role model for others.

Ron demonstrated his integrity, set an example, set the goals and objectives clearly, communicated clearly from time to time, connected with various stakeholders by building bridges, breaking barriers, and removing bottlenecks. He encouraged, supported, and inspired his people to transform the educational institution, which was on the verge of collapse, to greater heights of success. Hence, Ron was indeed a transformational leader.

From this case study, it becomes clear that right leadership is needed to lead an organization to success. This particular situation called for transformational leadership for saving the college from closing down, protecting the jobs of the employees, and providing quality education to the students.

To conclude, leaders have to act according to the situation, with more emphasis on transformational leadership, for taking their people and the organization to achieve their goals and objectives.

20

Build Leaders around You

"Before you are a leader, success is all about growing yourself. When you become a leader, success is all about growing others."

Jack Welch

Good leaders can become great leaders only when they help the people around them to develop as leaders. Every leader has a duty to develop successors who can take his position and enhance organizational effectiveness. In this chapter we will discuss how to develop leaders around you.

Organizations realize the importance of building leaders. They have their own programmes to develop leaders by identifying them early and grooming them. For instance, Procter and Gamble runs a leadership development programme called "Inspirational Leadership" and American Express has a programme called "Leadership Inspiring Employee Engagement". Similarly, many companies have leadership development programmes for their managers.

Ram Charan's Leaders At All Levels

Ram Charan highlighted the building of succession and leadership development from the ground up in his book

Leaders At All Levels. He mentioned the tools to spot the hidden leaders within the company at an early stage. He talked of measuring the "leadership talent deficit" in an organization and then making efforts to reduce, if not eliminate it; developing effective leaders through apprenticeship; recognizing leadership potential; customizing growth plan for each leader; explaining the crucial role of bosses; managing apprenticeship initiatives and relationships; selecting the CEO candidates early and grooming them; and institutionalizing the Apprenticeship Model.

Ram Charan describes how Jeff Immelt of GE would pore over a list of 175 top leaders of his company every day, thinking about where they fit, what they can do, and who needs to go to another job soon.

While building leaders it is essential to emphasize on the strengths of the people rather than on what they lack, as you cannot force anyone who is not good in a particular area to perform in that areas.

Leaders can be developed at the workplace by mentoring, coaching, classroom teaching, and training. This is an ideal mix for developing leaders. Ram Charan says that while leadership cannot be taught in a classroom, a mix of educational experiences, classroom training, voracious reading, and rubbing shoulders with others in seminars can accelerate a leader's growth.

Jim Collins' Level 5 Leadership

According to Jim Collins there are 5 Levels of Leadership. Level 1 leaders are the ones who work at an individual level, by themselves. They are competent workers and deliver the results effectively. They make productive contributions through their talent, knowledge, skills, and good work habits.

When these individual, competent workers work in teams and deliver the results through teamwork, they are known as Level 2 leaders. They contribute to the achievement of group objectives and work effectively with others in a group setting.

Level 3 leaders are those who are competent managers and who lead the contributors in their teams effectively. They organize people and resources towards the effective and efficient pursuit of predetermined objectives.

Level 4 leaders are the leaders who lead the Level 3 leaders effectively. They catalyse commitment, pursue a clear and compelling vision vigorously, and stimulate the group to perform at high levels.

At the pinnacle are the Level 5 leaders who build enduring greatness through a combination of personal humility and professional will. They lead their groups without expecting any rewards. They are highly passionate and take the blame in case of failure but give the credit to others in case of success. These Level 5 leaders also develop leaders around them.

John Maxwell's 5 Levels of Leadership

Though Maxwell's theory of 5 Levels of Leadership may appear to be similar to Jim Collins theory, it is actually quite different.

John Maxwell outlines *5 Levels of Leadership* based on his 30 years of experience in leadership development. He says that success in one position leads to successively higher positions in leadership, paving the way for individual and group development. This is a little similar to Abraham Maslow's theory of Hierarchy of Needs which says that after satisfying one level of need, individuals will try to satisfy the next higher level.

According to Maxwell, there are 5 levels of leadership. These are position, permission, production, people development, and pinnacle, which are closely associated with rights, relationships, results, reproduction, and respect respectively. After stabilizing and consolidating one level, you can go to the next higher level.

Build Leaders around You

In the first level of *position*, people follow you as you are designated as a leader. You will be able to influence others because of your position in the organization. In the second level of *permission*, people follow you as they are convinced about your credentials, success, and leadership. In the third level of *production*, people follow you as you have produced results and contributed to the organization. In the fourth level of *people development*, people follow you as you have developed others as leaders. Finally, in the fifth level of *pinnacle*, people follow you as you symbolize and represent true leadership. Maxwell says that less than 1 percent of people will be able to reach Level 5—The Pinnacle.

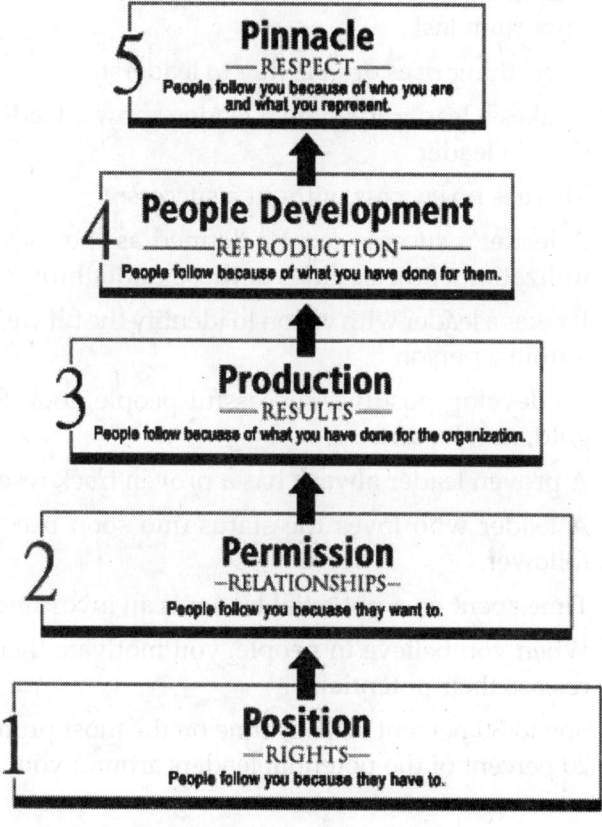

John Maxwell, in his book titled *Developing the Leaders around You*, says that great leaders help others reach their full potential by identifying and training potential leaders around them. Maxwell's dedication of an entire book on building others as leaders indicates the importance of building leaders. He says that Napoleon Bonaparte was one of history's greatest leaders. One of Napoleon's leadership secrets was knowing the needs of his men. He first determined what his men wanted most. Then he did everything possible to help them get it. He knew this was a key to successful motivation. Here are the key takeaways from Maxwell's book:

- Grow a leader—grow the organization.
- Acquiring and keeping good people is a leader's most important task.
- Everything rises or falls due to leadership.
- It takes a leader to know a leader, grow a leader, and show a leader.
- There is no success without a successor.
- A leader's success can be defined as the maximum utilization of the abilities of those under him.
- It takes a leader with vision to identify the future leader within a person.
- To develop positive, successful people, look for the gold, not the dirt.
- A proven leader always has a proven track record.
- A leader who loves the status quo soon becomes a follower.
- Time spent on a potential leader is an investment.
- When you believe in people, you motivate them and release their potential.
- Spend 80 percent of your time on the most promising 20 percent of the potential leaders around you.

- Give opportunities, resources, and playing time according to the players' past performance.
- People become empowered when you provide them with three things: opportunity, freedom, and security.
- A leader who produces other leaders multiplies his influence.
- Give your leaders deep, broad roots by growing them slowly and varying their experiences.
- Managers are maintainers and tend to rely on systems and controls. Leaders are innovators and creators who rely on people.
- True success comes only when every generation continues to develop the next generation.

Maxwell conveys an emphatic message in the book that leaders, who don't develop people will, one day, find themselves becoming unsuccessful. No matter how efficient and strategic they are, eventually they will fail.

Build Leaders around You

Prepare a list of people whom you want to develop as leaders. Every day invest some time on grooming them. Work for and share your knowledge with both volunteer and social groups. Peter Drucker was successful because he learned a lot while working for non-profit institutions. His experiences there helped him to develop his theories and become the father of modern management. He influenced Frances Hesselbein, Marshall Goldsmith, and many others. Hence, Drucker was a great leader who developed others as leaders.

Here are some tips to build leaders around you:
- Have trust in the members of your group
- Praise publicly and criticize privately
- Involve yourself intensively in the work
- Encourage the cream to rise to the top.

- Be passionate in making a difference to the lives of others. Deliver results without any expectations.

Charismatic leaders don't develop leaders as they believe in promoting themselves. They want people to feel their absence. When we look at leaders like Alexander the Great, Ashoka, and Genghis Khan, we see that they grew to become charismatic leaders. When they died, there was total disarray, resulting in the disintegration of their empires. Developing successors and others as leaders is essential for any organization.

21

Live Your Life Completely

"There isn't any Nobel Prize for management thinking. But it's just as well because it would have been won every year by the same man—Peter Drucker."

Geoffrey Colvin,
Editor, Fortune Magazine

Leaders must learn to live complete lives and balance their personal, professional, and social work. However, many present day leaders don't have time for their families, friends, or for social activities. Life loses its meaning when the focus is solely on professional work, ignoring the personal and social activities.

Peter Drucker is known as the father of modern management, but when we look at his biography, it is obvious that he led a complete life. He spent time not only for the cause of modern management, but also on social activities and hobbies like walking, swimming, writing, and mountain hiking. In this chapter we will see what we can learn from Peter Drucker about leading a meaningful and complete life.

Peter Drucker— A Brief Profile

Peter Drucker juggled multiple careers. He was a successful teacher, writer, and consultant. He wrote more than forty books and hundreds of articles in newspapers, magazines, and journals. In 2002, President George W. Bush awarded him the Presidential Medal of Freedom, America's highest civilian honour.

Peter Drucker

He said he had learnt a lot while teaching students. He stayed in contact with many of his students long after they had graduated. Many phoned or visited him. He was wise, but tough minded. He was good humoured, yet serious and profound when the need arose. He was capable of introspection, yet his focus was always on others. Throughout his life he was learning, unlearning, and relearning. Even in old age, Drucker had a lot of physical stamina. One of the reasons he gave for his longevity was the need to keep up with the pace set by his wife, Doris!

Drucker was a great visionary who forecasted the increase in the number of knowledge workers. He created several concepts, including MBO (management by objectives). He influenced many thinkers such as Marshall Goldsmith and Frances Hesselbein. Both Hamel and Prahalad acknowledged Drucker's contribution by saying that he was a person "whose wisdom has benefitted our work enormously."

In *The Effective Executive*, Drucker set out four rules for setting priorities. These are: focus on the future, not the past; focus on opportunities, not problems; don't climb on bandwagons and forget safe options; and aim high, at "something that will make a difference".

Drucker said that ethics and integrity are the key to effective leadership. People might forgive leaders for their mistakes, but not for their lack of integrity. He had a great respect for non-profit institutions. He believed in transformational rather than transactional leadership style.

Peter Drucker—Effective Manager of his Time

Peter Drucker had a diverse set of interests, activities, and pursuits but performed his basic activities of writing, teaching, and consulting for many years through a judicious use of his time. He did not take on activities, no matter how attractive, that would divert his attention from his core competencies. This meant turning down numerous offers to lecture, write forewords to books, and consult for organizations worldwide.

He remarked, "To lead a satisfying life in more than one world, you'll have to create the time to accomplish what you want."

Leadership Lessons from Drucker

There are a number of lessons we can learn from Peter Drucker to help us to become better leaders. Here are a few of them:

- Follow your passions and lead a complete life
- Manage your time
- Focus on your core competencies
- Differentiate between persistence and futility
- Reinvent yourself constantly
- Focus on achievement rather than making money
- Spend time on community service and work for non-profit institutions as it widens your mental horizons

- Never put off your work for the next day as every day is a good day to finish your work
- Learn to live in an imperfect world and strive to make it perfect
- Pursue your passions at every stage of your life
- You can work from anywhere if your knowledge is portable
- Abandon old practices systematically
- Treat employees as assets
- Focus on the customer
- Leave a legacy for tomorrow

Parallel Career

"Reinvention is bolder and more exciting than merely finding a new job, or deciding what one is going to do upon turning forty-five or sixty-five. It requires deep thought, creativity, the desire and ability to change, and the willingness to reach out to others." — Peter Drucker

Drucker once remarked, "We will have to learn to develop second careers for accomplished professional and managerial people when they reach their late forties or so." He was a good example of living a meaningful second half of life. He demonstrated that you don't necessarily have to change the things you do completely after the age of forty—just modify them suitably. He continued with his activities of writing, teaching, and consulting. The majority of his books were written after he turned sixty-five. But, as he got older, he made adjustments. He decreased his teaching load and only took on those consulting clients who were willing to travel to his home in Claremont, California.

Having skills in multiple areas provides stability to your career, apart from providing meaning to your life. If there is any downturn in one area, you can work in other areas.

Diverse skills also contribute to being a well rounded and a more interesting person. In *Management Challenges for the 21st Century*, Drucker wrote that a key tenet of self-management is developing a second major interest in life, preferably early in your career. Thus there are several benefits of having multiple interests.

Achieve Your Goals Joyfully

In our efforts to achieve our goals, we must remember not to sacrifice current happiness for the sake of future achievement. We need to strike a balance between current pressures and pleasures. Souza said, "Happiness is a journey not a destination." Hence, don't lose so much for so little. God has given us one life and we are not sure if we will get another one. We should do what we like to do, according to our passions and interests, so that we lead a successful and balanced personal, professional, and social life.

Drucker says that if the only goal in life is to make money, it will not lead to happiness. "I've known quite a few people," he said, "whose main goal was to make money. And they all made it.... If you are single-minded, focused on making money, you'll make money.... And without exception, they were all utterly miserable. They reached their goal, and there was nothing left."

Einstein said, "Try to be a person of value rather than a person of success." Hence, don't go looking for stones and leave the gems at home. Don't search for future happiness and ignore the present happiness. Don't run behind success. Make sure that success runs behind you. Lead your life completely by pursuing your passions and interests so that you do not have any regrets on your deathbed.

22

Make a Difference to the Lives of Others

"Lives of great men all remind us
We can make our lives sublime,
And, departing, leave behind us
Footprints on the sands of time."
                          Henry Wadsworth Longfellow

Leaders must maintain values, principles, and ethics. They must be an example for others to follow. They must not only add value to themselves, but also to the lives of others and also to future generations. In this chapter we will discuss about making a difference to the lives of others.

The actions leaders take must be for the good of others so that the society in which they live is benefitted. They can serve the society in many ways, for example, by giving charity or by spending their time on charitable activities. Leaders like Peter Drucker and Frances Hesselbein contributed to non-profit organizations and made a significant difference to the societies they lived in. Business leaders like Bill Gates and Warren Buffet contribute to the society through donations to the Bill and Melinda Gates Foundation. It requires a generous heart to help other people.

Corporate Social Responsibility

Corporate Social Responsibility (CSR) says that corporations have a responsibility towards the society. In addition to providing returns to shareholders, giving salaries to employees, paying interest to lenders, providing benefits to customers and suppliers, and paying taxes to the government, companies contribute to the society though sponsoring non-government, non-profit organizations and contributing to charities.

Mahatma Gandhi strongly espoused the concept of trusteeship. He said, "Supposing I have come by a fair amount of wealth, either by way of legacy or by means of trade and industry, I must know that all that wealth does not belong to me. What belongs to me is the right to an honourable livelihood, no better than that enjoyed by a million others. The rest of my wealth belongs to the community and must be used for the welfare of the community."

Individual Social Responsibility

"Charity given out of duty without expectation of return at the proper time and place and to a worthy person is considered to be in the mode of goodness." — Bhagavad Gita

Just like corporates, individuals have social responsibility too. This can be called Individual Social Responsibility (ISB), where individuals contribute towards the welfare of society. For instance, some people sponsor the education of a child, or donate to old age homes, or for development of slums, or to orphanages, and so on. Some people do voluntary work. Individuals are happier and have a sense of real achievement when they contribute something towards the welfare of the society.

Frances Hesselbein

Frances Hesselbein was the CEO of Girl Scouts of USA, the largest organization of girls and women in the world, from 1976-1990. Besides being an outstanding leader of non-profit organizations, she has a continued commitment to develop leaders of all ages. She was awarded the Presidential Medal of Freedom, the United States of America's highest civilian honour, in 1998. She has been influenced by Peter Drucker, the management legend and Marshall Goldsmith the coaching legend. She is the President and CEO of The Frances Hesselbein Leadership Institute (formerly the Peter F. Drucker Foundation for Nonprofit Management). She said, "Leadership is a matter of how to be, not how to do it." She received accolades from Peter Drucker who called her the world's best leader.

Frances Hesselbein
—Living Peter Drucker

She has received many honours for her contributions to Girl Scouts and leadership, such as USA's Lifetime Achievement Award and the International Leadership Association's Lifetime Achievement Award in 2008. She is the recipient of over 20 honorary degrees, and her work on leadership and management is respected globally. Marshall Goldsmith praised Frances Hesselbein saying, "In the world of leadership she is the role model." International leadership gurus such as Jim Collins, Warren Bennis, and Peter Senge have all praised her as an inspiring and thought leader.

She is not only an American icon but also an international one. She is a remarkable leader who made a difference to the lives of others through her contributions. She is a gracious woman leader, a servant leader, and a thought leader. We can say that she is the living Peter Drucker. Her actions will inspire all of us to work and contribute without looking for any rewards.

Warren E. Buffett and Bill Gates

Warren E. Buffett, the Chairman of Berkshire Hathaway Inc. and one of the world's wealthiest men, donated the bulk of his $44 billion fortune to the Bill and Melinda Gates Foundation. Out of his wealth, he presented the biggest donation to Gates, and $1 billion donations to his own foundation and to the foundations run by each of his three children. He said, "I am not an enthusiast for dynastic wealth, particularly when the alternative is 6 billion people having much poorer hands in life than we have." He says, "There is more than one way to get to heaven, but this is a great way."

Warren Buffett

Make a Difference

Many people want to make a difference to the lives of others, but don't know where to start. Here are some small things you can do to start with:

- Compliment people by highlighting their sincere efforts. It boosts their self-esteem and self-confidence. Don't indulge in artificial praise or else you will lose your credibility. Your compliment should be objective, specific, and should be given as soon as you notice the positive behaviour.
- Gift something to others such as stationery, flowers, books, or other small things. It makes the recepient feel important and they develop a positive attitude towards others.
- Have patience, care, and respect for others. Give something back to society either through money or through your services.
- And, above all, develop an attitude of gratitude towards the good others do to you.

In today's world, most of the people are caught up in the "I, me, myself" syndrome and "What's-in-it-for-me?" mindset, despite the fact that giving has been deeply ingrained in our socio-cultural psyche. It is essential to work hard to cultivate the attitude of giving something to society. Whether other people acknowledge your efforts or not, you must deliver your best as an individual. Just as many small drops make a mighty ocean, many small efforts can make a major difference to the society and to the world.

If leaders had not made sacrifices in the past, our world would have been worse off than what it is today. If we want our future generations to live in a better world, then we must contribute our best to the welfare of the society, without expecting anything in return. We must believe that *making a difference* is an investment for the benefit of our future generations.

23

Soar like an Eagle

"A smart man makes a mistake, learns from it, and never makes that mistake again. But a wise man finds a smart man and learns from him how to avoid the mistake altogether."

Roy H. Williams

We have discussed several rules for smart leadership in the previous chapters. In this concluding chapter we will look at a few more.

Lose a Battle to Win a War

At times it is essential to lose a battle in the short run, to win the war in the end. The American General George Washington lost several battles initially but won the war in the end. Similarly, Romans lost many battles when Hannibal attacked Italy, but finally won the war against him.

Hold Hope High

Sir Winston Churchill, who was called the "British Bulldog", never gave up during World War II. He encouraged his people and kept their hopes alive during the darkest hours of world history. He remarked, "Hope has always been the greatest weapon for England." He was instrumental in defeating Hitler and winning the war and exhorted his people, "Never give in! Never give in! Never give in! Never!"

Stand Up and Fight

Leaders must learn lessons from their failures and make sure that they don't repeat the same mistakes. Leaders must know how to stand up and fight. But they must know when to quit as well. They must not look back and regret their failures. They must learn their lessons and move on.

The road to success is covered with a lot of heartburns, hardships, and failures. Bill Walsh, former head coach and General Manager of the San Francisco 49ers, says, "Not every leader has the guts to get back in the game. A hard hit thins the crowd. If you can stand up and fight, you accomplish the most important thing you need to do." He had passion for winning and advised to expect defeats in life, to allow yourself some time for recovery; and plan your next move. He also believed in quitting graciously when time came. Leaders must learn to stand up and fight and also learn to quit graciously.

Be an Eagle

"Celebrate your success and stand strong when adversity hits, for when the storm clouds come in, the eagles soar while the small birds take cover." — Author Unknown

Justin Menkes, author of *Better Under Pressure* identifies three key attributes, that is, realistic optimism, subservience to purpose, and finding order in chaos, which allow great leaders to realize their potential and that of their people. And Gary Burnison, CEO of Korn/Ferry International reveals in his book, *No Fear of Failure*, "All leaders exhibit tremendous courage around the possibility, and even the inevitability at times, of failure. In the face of uncertainty, they draw on an inner strength that allows them to strive for what is possible rather than become paralysed by the risk of failure."

Eagles exhibit similar courage, tenacity, and soar high without any concern or fear of failure. We will discuss the concept by giving analogies of animals.

Turtles are considered to have low goals and low relationship. Sharks have high goals but low relationship. Teddy bears have high relationships but low goals. The relationship and goals for a fox is medium. It is only the eagles that have high relationship and high goals. Eagles stand out from the rest of the birds and animals because of their unique and extraordinary qualities. This is the reason why eagles stand for leadership.

Eagles are used as a symbol of visionary leadership. They can see any object from a long distance. They can also directly look into the sun, which is not possible for an average human being. Eagles use storms to fly higher and thus know how to convert threats into opportunities, while other birds take cover during storms. They represent thinking big, dreaming big, and daring big. They never settle for less. They want the best of everything in life. They are highly focused on their prey.

You have learnt several lessons in this book. These lessons will help you to minimize mistakes and maximize your leadership effectiveness and lead you to success. Now it is time to customize these lessons according to your attitude and capabilities because what worked for others may not work for you, as the times would have changed and people would be different. However, you can always apply the basic concepts you have learnt in this book when you face new challenges.

What Got You Here, Won't Get You There

Marshall Goldsmith in his book, *What Got You Here, Won't Get You There—How Successful People, Become Even More Successful!* reveals that you need to learn continuously, take feedback regularly, identify the barriers to reach your next higher level, and acquire new tools and techniques constantly to soar like an eagle.

Life is great!

Marshall Goldsmith

"I shall pass this way but once. Therefore any good that I can do, or any kindness that I can show, let me do it now for I shall not pass this way again."

William Penn

Bibliography

Adair, John, *Inspiring Leadership*
Axelrod, Alan, *Eisenhower on Leadership: Ike's Enduring Lessons in Total Victory Management*
Burnison, Gary, *No Fear of Failure*
Charan, Ram, *Leaders At All Levels*
Charan, Ram, *Leadership in the Era of Economic Uncertainty: The New Rules for Getting the Right Things Done in Difficult Times*
Collins, Jim, *Good to Great*
Covey, Stephen R., *The Seven Habits of Highly Effective People*
Deccan Chronicle October 30, 2011, *The Ultimate Insider*
Drucker, Peter, *The Effective Executive*
Drucker, Peter, *Management Challenges for the 21st Century*
Finkelstein, Sydney and Eric M., *Immunity from Implosion—Building Smart Leadership*
Goldsmith, Marshall, *What Got You Here Won't Get You There—How Successful People Become Even More Successful*
Maxwell, John C., *5 Levels of Leadership*
Maxwell, John C., *Developing the Leaders Around You*
Maxwell, John C., *Success – What Every Leader Needs to Know*
Menkes, Justin, *Better Under Pressure*
Nocera, Joe, Running GE, *Comfortable in His Skin*, New York Times, June 9, 2007, p. C9

Nye Jr, Joseph S., *The Powers to Lead*

Peshawaria, Rajeev, *Too Many Bosses, Too Few Leaders: The Three Essential Principles You Need to Become an Extraordinary Leader*

Rao, M. S., *Spot Your Leadership Style, Build Your Leadership Brand*

Rosenstein, Bruce, *Living in More Than One World: How Peter Drucker's Wisdom Can Inspire and Transform Your Life*

Rosentein, Bruce, *Transform your lives*

Rowe, W. Glenn, *Cases in Leadership*

Rudan, Gina, *Practical Genius*

Urwick, Lester, *Elements of Administration*

Walsh, Bill, Steve Jamison, and Craig Walsh, *The Score Takes Care of Itself: My Philosophy of Leadership*

Online References

Author's Blog: profmsr.blogspot.com

Author's Blog: professormsraoguru.blogspot.com

mlknationalparade.org/

www.darpanmagazine.com/2011/09/darpans-last-words-2011-september-october-issue/

www.accessmylibrary.com/article-1G1-14922906/leadership-and-vision-importance.html

www.thehindubusinessline.in/2006/07/28/stories/2006072801571100.htm

www.religion-online.org/showarticle.asp?title=1522

www.thepracticeofleadership.net/are-you-a-leader-or-just-a-boss

Glossary

360 Degree Feedback	:	This is the feedback taken from all sources, such as superiors, suppliers, subordinates, peers, clients, and others.
Blind Spots	:	The weaknesses about themselves that people don't know about.
Business Acumen	:	It is the ability to spot and exploit business opportunities.
Catalytic Leader	:	This is a leader who has the knack of leading a diverse group of people effectively by managing their egos, emotions, and feelings, thus effecting change successfully.
Comfort Zone	:	It is the zone where people, who prefer to stay away from risk, remain. Usually these people are non-achievers.
Effective Zone	:	It is the zone where achievers and potential achievers prefer to remain. They enjoy taking risk and make big achievements in their lives.
Expert Power	:	It is the power to influence others through knowledge, skills, and abilities.
Hard Leadership	:	It is a leadership style where leaders emphasize more on tasks and less on people. This style is useful in handling unskilled workers. However, this style is not appreciated by the team members and should be used sparingly.

Hard Power	: It is the method of getting outcomes through inducements, rewards, or threats of punishment.
Hard Skills	: These are the skills related to technical competence and are about domain skills.
Innovative Leadership	: This is an unconventional style of leadership where leaders adopt out-of-the-box approach to achieve their organisational objectives.
Leadership Talent Deficit	: It is a scenario where there is a dearth of leadership talent within the organisation.
Legitimate Power	: The power people have legally.
Level 5 Leaders	: The term was coined by Jim Collins in his book, *Good to Great* where leaders possess a blend of professional will and personal humility. These leaders are highly passionate and don't mind if someone else takes the credit for their contributions.
Myth Makers	: The people who create myths or mythical situations.
Negative Zone	: This is the toxic and unproductive zone that saps energy.
Network	: It helps people to connect with others. It aligns the right people to the right positions, thus achieving the desired objectives.
People Acumen	: It is the ability to understand the concerns of the people and the ability to handle them well.
Plan A, Plan B, Plan C	: It is about keeping alternative plans ready for execution if a particular plan fails.
Positional Power	: The power that people have due to their official positions.

Proactive Paranoia	:	It is the obsession to take initiative and being proactive in nature.
Professional will	:	This term is used by Jim Collins in his book, *Good to Great* to describe the behaviour of people who are committed and dedicated towards their work. When professional will and personal humility go together, then it is known as Level 5 Leadership.
Referent Power	:	The power that people have even though they do not have any organisational affiliations.
Smart Leaders	:	These leaders blend soft and hard power and soft and hard skills to achieve the desired outcomes.
SMART Goals	:	It is the acronym for **s**pecific, **m**easurable, **a**chievable, **r**eachable, and **t**rackable goals.
Smart Means	:	These are the means adopted to achieve the goals where more of brain power and less of brawn power is involved.
Smart Methods	:	The methods that give quick and quality results.
Smart Work	:	It is the ability to put in efforts to get the things done by keeping both means and ends in mind. It involves more of systematic planning and emphasizes qualitative inputs and efforts.
Soft Leadership	:	It is a term coined to describe a leadership style where leaders emphasize soft tactics and soft power to get the tasks executed successfully. It involves people orientation, but without losing focus on tasks.
Soft Power	:	It is the method of getting the outcomes by attracting and persuading rather than by coercing and manipulating.

Soft Skills	:	These are the skills, abilities and traits related to one's personality, attitude, and behaviour.
Tale Tellers	:	The people who have the art of telling stories to communicate with others.
Task Orientation	:	It is an attitude where people emphasize more on tasks rather than on people.
Transformational Attitude	:	It is the attitude of persons with people orientation who get the tasks executed successfully in a manner that makes a difference to the lives of others.
Transformational Leaders	:	The leaders who bring out changes within the system. They have people-orientation.
Transactional Attitude	:	It is an attitude of task orientation to get the tasks executed successfully. This attitude is not widely appreciated.
Transactional Leaders	:	These leaders emphasize more on ends rather than means. They have more of work orientation, rather than people orientation.
Visionary Leadership	:	This leadership involves setting a broad vision and articulating it effectively to achieve the goals and objectives.
Win-Lose	:	It is an aggressive style where one person wins at the cost of others.
Win-Win	:	It is an assertive and collaborative approach where all the contending parties are happy with the outcome while resolving the conflicts. It is an ideal conflict resolution style. However, it takes a lot of time and is not easy to implement.
Wise Work	:	It is a blend of hard work and smart work to achieve the desired outcomes.

Index

360 degree feedback 26

Adair, John 129
Allen, James 29
Angell, Dr James R. 27
Aristotle 39
Articulate 3, 28, 29, 30, 31, 34, 37, 106
Axelrod, Alan 129

Bass, Bernard M. 101, 106
Beethoven 3
Bennis, Warren ix, 101, 122
Benson, Ezra Taft 91
Bin Laden, Osama 15, 16, 17, 18, 19, 20
Blanchard, Ken 78
Blind spots 78, 131
Boss 24, 25, 26, 27, 75, 109, 130
Branson, Sir Richard 34, 36
Brennan, John O. 20
Brothers, Dr Joyce 9
Buffett, Warren 32, 120, 123
Burns, James McGregor xiii, 45, 100, 101
Bush, George W. 17, 116
Bush, Vannevar 57

Caine, Michael 53
Calm leaders 54, 56, 93
Carnegie, Andrew 69
Carnegie, Dale 13
Carter, Jimmy 17
Catalytic leader 20, 131
Charan, Ram xix, 50, 86, 108, 109, 129
Charismatic 40, 41, 42, 45, 53, 101, 114
Chiesi, Danielie 44
Churchill, Winston 53, 54, 125
Coercive power 41, 42
Collins, Jim xix, 6, 20, 63, 70, 89, 94, 109, 110, 122, 129, 132, 133

Colvin, Geoffrey 115
Comfort zone 6, 8, 131
Communicate 3, 5, 9, 10, 11, 28, 29, 30, 31, 32, 34, 37, 57, 66, 70, 72, 82, 83, 85, 103, 104, 106, 134
Cook, Timothy 40
Coolidge, Calvin 8
Core competencies 99, 117
Covey, Stephen 10, R. 97, 129
Crafted strategy xv
Creativity 5, 12, 12, 14, 32, 39, 51, 71, 118

Dalai Lama 6, 46, 88
Davies, Peter Maxwell 81
Delegate viii, 60, 62, 66, 67, 68, 69, 70, 71, 72, 76
Dell, Michael 4, 5, 36
DePree, Max 92
Donilon, Thomas 20
Drucker, Peter xix, 21, 77, 98, 99, 100, 113, 115, 116, 117, 118, 119, 120, 122, 123, 129, 130
Dyer, Wayne 37

Eagle Claw, operation 17
Ebbers, Bernie 45
Edison, Thomas Elva 39
Effective zone 6, 8, 131
Einstein, Albert 55, 119
Ellison, Larry 36
Emerson 8
Empower viii, 18, 67, 68, 74, 75, 76, 77, 113
Ends 43, 44, 45, 46, 47, 48, 101, 134, 135
EQ 86
Eric M. 5, 129
Ethics 43, 45, 46, 47, 77, 90, 101, 117, 120
Eustress 57
Ewing, Russell H. 25

Excellence 15, 19, 22, 25, 38, 39, 41, 74, 84
Expert power 42, 131

Feedback 4, 26, 34, 61, 70, 76, 78, 79, 80, 81, 82, 83, 88, 90, 105, 128, 131, 136
Feedback, informal 81
Feedback, sandwich 82, 83, 105
Finkelstein, Sydney 129
Fleming xvi
Fowler, Raymond D. 78
Fox, Vicente 90
Franklin, Benjamin 97
French, John 41
Fromm, Erich 52
Frost, Robert 35

Gates, Bill 36, 120, 121, 123
Geronimo, operation 15, 16, 18, 19, 54
Getty, J. Paul 49
Giannini, Amadeo P. 55
Giuliani, Rudolph Rudy 53, 55, 56, 57
Goldsmith, Marshall xx, 78, 90, 113, 116, 122, 128, 129
Goleman, Daniel 84
Grant, Ulysses S. 77
Greenleaf, Robert 93
Groupthink 5

Hard asset 6, 12
Hard leader 6, 40, 132
Hard power 5, 6, 7, 132, 133
Hard skill viii, ix, 5, 7, 84, 85, 86, 132, 133
Hawke, Bob 34
Hesselbein, Frances 95, 113, 116, 120, 122
Hitler 6, 46, 126
Humility 5, 20, 48, 70, 88, 89, 90, 91, 94, 110, 132, 133
Hyles, Jack 74

Ides, Carole Nicola 86
Immelt, Jeff 4, 5, 40, 109
Individual social responsibility 121
Information overload 14, 62, 63
Innovate 5, 32, 35, 36, 39, 40, 41, 42, 51, 113, 132
Innovative leadership 36, 41
Insider trading 44
IQ 84, 86

Jackson, Eric M. 5
Jamison, Steve 130
Jefferson, Thomas 15
Jobs, Steve xix, 4, 5, 32, 35, 36, 37, 38, 39, 40, 41, 42,

Kanter, Rosabeth Moss 29
Kennedy, John F. 23, 30, 31, 34, 97
Kiam, Victor 47
King Jr, Martin Luther xix, 1, 2, 3, 23, 30, 31, 34, 42, 46
Kouzes, James 28
Kozlowski, L. Dennis 45
Kyi, Aung San Suu 34, 46

Law, Vernon Sanders xix
Leadership talent deficit 109
Legitimate power 26, 42, 132
Level 5 leader 6, 20, 70, 89, 94, 109, 110, 132, 133
Lincoln, Abraham 23, 53, 55, 56, 77, 79, 89, 97
Longfellow, Henry 96
Longfellow, Henry Wadsworth 120

Mahatma Gandhi 2, 23, 30, 31, 34, 42, 43, , 46, 88, 99, 121
Manage change 50
Manager vii, xi, 5, 28, 44, 77, 81, 98, 108, 110, 113, 117, 118, 126
Mandino, Og 4
Maslow, Abraham 69, 110
Maxwell, John xix, 22, 62, 74, 98, 110, 111, 112, 113, 129
MBO 116
McCloy, John J. 91
Means 2, 3, 6, 11, 35, 38, 43, 44, 45, 46, 47, 48, 66, 77, 92, 101, 133, 134, 135
Menkes, Justin 126, 129
Mental time 60
Michelangelo 3
Mintzberg, Henry xv
Mission 15, 28, 40, 47, 95
Moffat, Robert 44
Motivation 3, 5, 29, 31, 72, 85, 100, 104, 106, 112
Myth makers 101, 132

Nanus 101
Negative zone 64, 132
Network 6, 9, 10, 11, 34, 44, 72, 133

Index

Nightingale, Florence xix, 46, 92, 93, 94, 95
Nocera, Joe 129
Nooyi, Indra 98
Nye Jr., Joseph 130

Obama, Barack xix, 13, 15, 16, 17, 18, 19, 20, 54

Panetta, Leon 20
Parallel career 118
Passion 12, 20, 33, 37, 38, 39, 40, 94, 95, 110, 114, 117, 118, 119, 126, 132
Patton, George S. 71
Peale, Norman Vincent 93
People acumen 86, 133
Persevere 13, 36, 39
Peshawaria, Rajeev 25, 130
Plan A, Plan B, Plan C 52, 57, 133
Popular 21, 22, 23, 56,
Posner, Barry 28
Proactive paranoia 5, 133
Professional will 6, 20, 89, 94, 110, 132, 133

Rajaratnam, Raj 44
Raven, Bertam 41
Referent power 26, 41, 42, 133
Reward power 42
Roosevelt, Elanor 30, 95
Roosevelt, Theodore 24, 66
Rosenstein, Bruce 130
Rowe, W. Glenn 130
Rudan, Gina 12, 130

Schweitzer, Albert 45
Scully, John 32
Servant, servant leader viii, x, xi, 92, 93, 94, 95, 122
Shakespeare 3
Skilling, Jeff 44
Slim, Carlos 55
Smart goals 133
Smart leaders vii, xv, xvi, xvii, xix, 4, 5, 6, 7, 125, 129, 133
Smart means 6, , 133
Smart work 5, 6, 10, 34, 63, 67, 134, 135
Soft asset 12, 14
Soft leader xix, 6, 33, 40, 134
Soft power 6, 134
Soft skill viii, ix, 14, 84, 85, 86, 134
Souza 119
Spurgeon, Charles H. 88
Stewart, Martha 44

Stewart, Potter 45
Sullivan, John 41
Synergy 10, 11

Tagore, Rabindranath 89
Tale tellers 101, 134
Tannen, Deborah ix
Task orientation 40, 134, 135
Tata, J. R. D. 47
Tata, Ratan 47
Team building 5, 38, 85
Teresa, Mother 42, 46, 88, 95
Time management 59, 60, 61, 64, 82, 85
Time wasters 60
Transactional attitude 25, 135
Transactional leadership xiii, 40, 101, 117, 135
Transformational attitude 25, 134
Transformational leader viii, xiii, 2, 30, 100, 101, 107, 135
Trompenaars, Fons vii
Turner, Anthea 67
Tzu, Lao 19, 84, 88
Tzu, Sun 89

Uncertainty 35, 49, 50, 51, 52, 54, 57, 59, 127, 129
Unethical 43, 48
Urwick, Lester 69, 130

Vision 3, 25, 28, 29, 30, 31, 32, 34, 36, 37, 38, 40, 41, 42, 47, 49, 77, 95, 106, 110, 112, 116, 127, 130, 135
Visionary leader 28, 32, 34, 36, 42, 127
Voltaire 64

Walsch, Neale Donald 68
Walsh, Bill 126, 130
Walsh, Craig 130
Weber, Max 101
Welch, Jack 5, 40, 108
Williams, Roy H. 125
Williamson, Marianne 11
Wilson, Woodrow 77
Win-lose 6, 135
Win-win 6, 10, 19, 67, 135
Wise work 34, 135

Yeltsin, Boris 53, 55, 56
Yoffie, Prof. David B. 40

Zuckerberg, Mark 36

A note to the reader

"The difference between school and life? In school, you are taught a lesson and then given a test. In life, you are given a test that teaches you a lesson."

Tom Bodett

I have written this book to describe leadership skills that can make you a smart leader. My aim is to help you to learn the lessons well so as to eliminate leadership failures and enhance your success as a leader. If this book helps you to achieve your goals, it would have done its job. If you put this book down feeling that you are better equipped to grow as a successful leader and make a difference to this world, I will believe that my work as an author has been successful.

I will appreciate your feedback to make improvements to this book. You may post your feedback at http://speakerwiki.org/speakers/Professor_MSRao or send an email to profmsr7@gmail.com. If you want information on the seminars and workshops on leadership that I conduct or my availability as a speaker for your group or conference, please contact me. You may also visit my blogs http://profmsr.blogspot.com and http://professormsraoguru.blogspot.com. These blogs pertain to Leadership Development, Soft Skills, Entrepreneurship, Corporate Training, Self-Improvement, and Personality Development. Please post your comments directly on the blogs themselves, as it helps others appreciate your ideas. If you find the blogs interesting, please share the link with your friends, as knowledge grows when shared.

You may share your thoughts about *Smart Leadership – Lessons for Leaders* on Facebook, Twitter, and the websites you visit. You can also blog about it or write a book review.

I pray for your success.

Professor M. S. Rao
Founder, *MSR Leadership Consultants India*